ANGLOPHONE CARIBBEAN POETRY, 1970–2001

ANGLOPHONE CARIBBEAN POETRY, 1970–2001

An Annotated Bibliography

Emily Allen Williams

Bibliographies and Indexes in World Literature, Number 57

GREENWOOD PRESS
Westport, Connecticut • London

Library of Congress Cataloging-in-Publication Data

Williams, Emily Allen.
   Angelophone Caribbean poetry, 1970–2001 : an annotated bibliography / Emily Allen
Williams.
     p. cm.—(Bibliographies and indexes in world literature, ISSN 0742–6801 ; no. 57)
   Includes bibliographical references and indexes.
   ISBN 0–313–31747–X (alk. paper)
   1. Caribbean poetry (English)—Bibliography. 2. West Indian poetry
(English)—Bibliography. 3. Caribbean Area—In literature—Bibliography. 4. West
Indies—In literature—Bibliography. I. Title. II. Series.
Z1524.P6W45   2002
[PR9205.2]
016.821'54099729—dc21   2002069617

British Library Cataloguing in Publication Data is available.

Library of Congress Catalog Card Number: 2002069617
ISBN: 0–313–31747–X
ISSN: 0742–6801

First published in 2002

Greenwood Press, 88 Post Road West, Westport, CT 06881
An imprint of Greenwood Publishing Group, Inc.
www.greenwood.com

Printed in the United States of America

The paper used in this book complies with the
Permanent Paper Standard issued by the National
Information Standards Organization (Z39.48–1984).

10 9 8 7 6 5 4 3 2 1

Contents

Preface

This bibliography is the product of my search for a concise reference on Caribbean Poetry. When I was writing my doctoral thesis five years ago, I was looking for a text that would give me a comprehensive overview of the poetry produced in the Anglophone Caribbean region from 1970 to the present (then 1997). While there were several references that, in combination, enabled me to piece together the *who* (the poets), the *what* (their individual works), the *where* (their geographical parameters), the *how* (aesthetics), and the *why* (theory), a single source that synthesized these areas of scholarly inquiry was unavailable. The few and very useful sources that did exist were generally limited to a catalogue of works by specific authors without the benefit of appended secondary sources. Usually, the timeframe or reference of these sources – either too limited or too ambitious – provided inadequate, as well as inaccurate, views of the scope of the literature and the poets working within the Anglophone Caribbean Poetry tradition. Furthermore, in these limited sources, there were simply listings of primary and secondary materials without the added benefit of annotations – annotations that often prove invaluable to the novice, as well as the more seasoned scholar and researcher. It was obvious to me in 1997, therefore, that even though there was an increased interest in the literature emanating from the Anglophone Caribbean, there was insufficient scholarly investigation of the poets and their artistry. This void, in part, can be attributed to the lack of access to and knowledge about background material and sources that [can] serve as "open" windows to information for the novice scholar and as treasure chests of "hidden" primary sources and critical views for the more seasoned scholar. Nevertheless, it is critically imperative *now* to uncover and present such material and sources toward an enhanced study and critical assessment of Anglophone Caribbean Poetry.

In the last decade, there has not been a *substantial annotated bibliography* that exclusively *yet* selectively *collects* and *annotates* the primary and secondary materials of the Anglophone Caribbean Poetry tradition. In his textual approach to the study of West Indian Poetry, *An Introduction to West Indian Poetry*, Laurence Breiner concurs, "Bibliographic research for West Indian Poetry is still in its infancy..." (xiii).[1] *Anglophone Caribbean Poetry, 1970-2001: An Annotated Bibliography*, then, is my attempt to bring together, in one publication, *select* anthologies, reference materials, conference proceedings, poet's individual collections, criticism, interviews, and recorded works for the period of 1970-2001.

The aim of *Anglophone Caribbean Poetry, 1970-2001: An Annotated Bibliography*, is to lead the audience (a combination of students, college and university professors, and independent scholars and researchers) beyond an embryonic stage of a mere listing together of a few major authors toward a more expansive view of the canon of Anglophone Caribbean Poetry. Toward such an end, this bibliography considers not only the poetry from 1970-2001 but its attendant criticism as well. Specifically, the materials in this text represent the ethos of the Independence Generation and Post Colonial Generation of writers from the Caribbean Basin Region and those writers working and living in the Caribbean Diaspora. Specifically, I have opted to include the poetry of writers born in the late thirties and through the 1940's, who established their careers in the 1960's and thereafter, the Independence Generation of Writers. Works by writers born in the 1950's and later, who became known in the 1970's through the present are also included, the Post Colonial Generation of Writers. The critical material has been gathered from a wide array of journals, casebooks, monographs, anthologies, and recorded materials.

The first criterion for selection of material for this bibliography was, of course, the accessibility of the material for review pursuant to the creation of annotations for each listed work. Each of the works listed has been thoroughly read (printed matter), viewed, and/or listened to (audio and audiovisual materials) in conjunction with the annotations that accompany each listing. Yet, it is important to stress that the annotations here are offered in an informational spirit more than in an evaluative one, as my major intent is to open pathways for scholars, researchers, and critics to render new readings and re-readings of texts both new and familiar to them and *not* to create fixed "readings" of texts. So, while some annotations may offer a critical remark or two, these remarks are meant to serve as guideposts not stop signs on the pathway of critical and analytical pursuit.

The poets included in this bibliography come from and live both inside and outside the Caribbean Basin Region. In collecting the materials for this text, the term *Anglophone Caribbean Poetry* is presented here to mean the work created by poets from the former British Caribbean territories, both island and mainland.[2] These territories include Anguilla, Antigua, Bahamas, Barbados, Barbuda, Belize, Bermuda, British Virgin Islands, Cayman Islands, Dominica, Grenada, Guyana, Jamaica, Montserrat, St. Kitts-Nevis, St. Lucia, St. Vincent, Turks and Caicos Islands, and Trinidad and Tobago. While the U. S. Virgin Islands have had no British affiliation, in reflecting as much of the artistry as possible of the English-speaking Caribbean, I have opted to include the works of poets from this area.

Every effort has been made to list the relevant authors and works germane to the Anglophone Caribbean Poetry tradition. Some works are not included here simply because they were not available to me [within the geographic and time limitations for the completion of this text] and not due to a lack of knowledge about their existence. Also, some works [just] published in 2000 and 2001 were not available to me before this text went to press. Two notable mentions in this category are Kamau Brathwaite's *Ancestors: A Reinvention of Mother Poem, Sun Poem, and X/Self* (2001) and *Words Need Love Too* (2000). On another note, some texts were out of print, which is one of the sad commentaries on the availability of a great deal of fine poetry in the Anglophone Caribbean literary canon. Most bibliographies clearly "feel their age," or are dated when they appear, and I, therefore, encourage all readers, scholars, and critics of Anglophone Caribbean Poetry to look closely for additional volumes of poetry published in the years 2000-2001. I am certain that omissions have been made along the pathway to the presentation of this text; consequently, I sincerely welcome comments and suggestions for the second edition of this text.

As you begin to turn these pages, it should become clear, however, that despite these limitations of accessibility, geography, and time, *Anglophone Caribbean Poetry, 1970-2001: An Annotated Bibliography*, is a substantial, annotated listing of the primary and secondary works in a rapidly growing literary tradition. The text has been organized into six annotated sections: I) Anthologies; II) References (Bibliographies, Dictionaries, and Indexes); III) Conference Proceedings; IV) Poets' (Individual) Collections; V) Criticism (Casebooks, Journal Essays, and Monographs); and VI) Interviews. Section VII lists Recorded Works and Section VIII is a Guide to Further Reading. This text also contains three indexes: Author, Title, and Subject. The numbers in the indexes refer to entry numbers, not page numbers, in the bibliography.

Anglophone Caribbean Poetry, 1970-2001: An Annotated Bibliography will lay another stone in the foundation toward the expansion of knowledge about the literature of the Anglophone Caribbean. Perhaps some of the conversations about the lack of knowledge of an Anglophone Caribbean Poetry tradition can be laid to rest by referring to this text. Concurrently, I hope that this annotated bibliography will "open the eyes" of the editors of many of the inaccurately titled "World Literature" texts to the literature, poetry specifically, that is being produced in the part of the world referred to variously as the Caribbean Basin Region, the Antilles, and the West Indies. Therefore, while all work can continue *ad infinitum*, I am offering this bibliography now not as an end but as a beginning toward generating a more focused and rigorous critical analysis of the poetry and a more refined understanding of the Anglophone Caribbean Poetry aesthetic.

Nothing is ever created or completed in isolation even though bibliographic work is extremely solitary – the solo reading and annotating. Yet, those hours of reading and annotating were made possible by the Main Library and Inter-Library

Loan staffs at the University of the West Indies/Mona Campus (Kingston, Jamaica) and Virginia Commonwealth University in Richmond, Virginia. I must thank the Council for the International Exchange of Scholars (CIES) and the Fulbright Foundation for a Fulbright Fellowship during the 2000-2001 academic year, which allowed me to be in residence at the University of the West Indies/Mona. Professors Mervyn Morris and Edward Baugh at the University of the West Indies were excellent sources of knowledge and support, providing books, names of writers, and valuable advice as I read and annotated.

Dr. George Butler, my editor at Greenwood, has shown me the way to assemble a well-planned bibliography. His instruction and patience are rare in a world that demands results yesterday, as he so graciously extended my deadline for submission as I made changes and corrections to this bibliography.

My husband, Kenneth, deserves thanks for his understanding as I placed myself in voluntary isolation many, many days. For my father, Joseph Allen, all the things I talked about as a child are beginning to happen. For everyone else, too many to name individually, thanks again and again.

---

[1] Breiner, Laurence. *An Introduction to West Indian Poetry*. Cambridge University Press, 1998.

[2] To refer to "poets from the Caribbean" without qualification is misleading. A number of the poets who I list in this text do not reside in the Caribbean Basin Region. "From" is used here to refer to poets that do, indeed, live in the region, those with birth ties to the region, and those who may have been born in Europe, [other areas of] North America, or Africa but yet have family ties to the Caribbean, hence a Caribbean sensibility in their writing.

Introduction

It is no longer possible, nor is it considered "academically correct" to isolate the study of Caribbean Literature to the margins of the global literary canon. It is essential that the publications of earlier period poets working within the Anglophone Caribbean literary tradition be gathered textually along with the publications of contemporary poets in order to assess the scope of the work, as well as to articulate a more grounded and sophisticated critical tradition of Caribbean Poetry Aesthetics. In the future, the most respected scholars and critics in this discipline undoubtedly will be those with lucid knowledge of the past poets, their literature, and its attendant criticism as well as knowledge of the work of contemporary poets and their critics.

In initiating a discourse about the past and present canon of Anglophone Caribbean Poetry, there are several departure points. In the introduction to their compilation, *The Oxford Book of Caribbean Short Stories*, Stewart Brown and John Wickham suggest that Caribbean Literature can be grouped into four "generations": The Pioneer Group born before the First World War and publishing in the years before the Second; the Nationalist Generation of writers born before the mid-1930's who were writing most vigorously in the decades approaching the Independence Period in the Caribbean; the Independence Generation of writers born in the late thirties and through the 1940's who established their writing careers in the sixties around and after that Independence Period; and the contemporary flowering of Post-Colonial writers born around 1950 or later, who came to prominence in the seventies and eighties, and are writing into the 1990's.[1]

This text, *Anglophone Caribbean Poetry, 1970-2001: An Annotated Bibliography*, includes a list of works that represents the ethos of the Independence and Post-Colonial Generation of writers. The list includes select poetry as well as its attendant criticism for a thirty-one year period beginning with the year 1970. This selection was made based on the centrality of several events, now historical, that were catalytic in changing the artistic and critical pace of production as well as the systematic scholarly inclusion and critical investigation of the literature in schools, colleges, and universities on an international scale.

The first event occurred in 1971 – a conference presented through the sponsorship of the Association for Commonwealth Literature and Language Studies (ACLALS). The focus of the conference was West Indian Literature and while the focus of the conference, in itself, was not novel, the location for the conference was a departure from its customary setting and, perhaps, changed the course of West Indian Literature for the remainder of the twentieth century. The conference was held at the University of the West Indies (UWI) on the Mona Campus in Kingston, Jamaica. This location was a far cry from the customary setting of past conferences, a British university. In placing the conference at UWI, ACLALS officials gave birth to an important historical event – the first assembly for the discussion of West Indian Literature by West Indian people on West Indian soil.

The opening session was seminal in the shaping and presentation of Caribbean Literature to a wider audience – a potential world audience – than the literature had theretofore been exposed to or embraced by. That opening session embodied a multi-dimensional literary tension out of which grew the beginnings of systematic critical examinations, as well as extended and innovative theorizing about the nature, premises, and purposes of West Indian literature. What emerges [in the reports from the conference] as most memorable, perhaps, are the lucidly adversative messages delivered by each of the panelists – (Edward) Kamau Brathwaite, Barbadian professor, historian and poet; V. S. Naipaul, East Indian/ Caribbean novelist; and Raja Rao, Indian novelist – at the opening session.

Brathwaite's address explored for the first time, in-depth, his concept of the "Little Tradition" – the culture of the ordinary people. In his address, he suggested that writers could move toward achieving a sense of cultural cohesiveness in the Caribbean Basin Region through a fundamental "re-education" of each racial and cultural entity [in the region] about its past before attempting to describe and analyze a present day multi-cultural Caribbean society. In his address, Brathwaite placed a major emphasis on historical identification with Africa as the template for understanding Caribbean folk culture. Most importantly, Brathwaite saw writers as being an integral part of society in their articulation of people's experiences and emotions toward cultural understanding. While V. S. Naipaul did not directly debate the major points articulated by Brathwaite, the essence of his address was one of antithesis.

Naipaul found the subject of the session, the function of the writer in society, to be out of touch with his conception of West Indian society's ability to sufficiently nurture and sustain creative activity. Stemming back to his historically infamous statement that "nothing was created in the West Indies," Naipaul's address to the conference focused on the writer's activity as one of self-cultivation, which necessarily moves the writer away from a society that (Naipaul believed) could not and would not provide the audiences necessary for the mental, emotional, and financial support of the writer. (His position in the latter part of the twentieth century became more moderate; he began to examine ways in which the writer might be able to function in tandem with his or her society).

Raja Rao, the third panelist, moved even further away from the prevailing subject of the session by asserting that the writer's primary aim was isolation if he or she aspired to create the most inspired and inspiring writing. His stance was clearly one of isolation in the writing process. While Rao was not familiar to as many attendees at the conference as they were with Brathwaite and Naipaul, those attendees that were familiar with George Lamming's writing and philosophy were not total strangers to Rao's philosophical position that the best writing takes place in a silent and alienated state.

While the messages of Brathwaite, Naipaul, and Rao created a charged literary atmosphere, more specifically, they sparked an inaugural dialectic in West Indian territory about West Indian literature and culture unlike that at previous conferences held at British universities. The presenters' messages in the opening session provided evidence of very different yet carefully critical platforms toward the expansion of the discourse on Caribbean Literature. Without question, Brathwaite, Naipaul, and Rao reached a much wider audience [toward the expansion of the scholarly activity in the discipline] than they and other individual writers or critics could have reached in the [then] widely read journals with a focus on Caribbean Literature.[2]

Another event in 1972 that dramatically changed the shape of Caribbean literature and caused the Anglo-Caribbean literary terrain to expand was the *Caribbean Festival of the Arts* (*Carifesta*) in Georgetown, Guyana. *Carifesta*, the first pan-Caribbean arts festival, provided opportunities for presentation, publication, and critical review on, perhaps, the largest scale ever in the Caribbean region. *Carifesta* was originally conceived as a regional festival that would encompass and give credence to all of the creative and artistic skills and energies, not only of the member countries of the CARICOM and the wider Caribbean, but also to the recognition, acceptance, and participation of those individuals living and working in the Caribbean Diaspora. Indeed, the first *Carifesta* (as well as subsequent ones) provided an unparalleled opportunity for the population of the Caribbean as well as the world to view, sample, and interact with a kaleidoscope of visual, literary, and performing arts and artists as well as a variety of culinary and indigenous arts and artists.

Notably, in the same year as *Carifesta*, Walcott's autobiographical poem, *Another Life*, an epic-scale work about the growth of the imagination, was published. From that point, a number of new poetic voices began to emerge from the Caribbean region and the Caribbean Diaspora, marking a generation informed and influenced by the Black Power Movement in the United States of America. Mervyn Morris, Anthony McNeill, Wayne Brown, Dennis Scott, and Faustin Charles emerge as the major poetic voices of the Post-Independence Era, the 1970's, complementing the major voices in the genre from the 1940's through the 1960's such as Derek Walcott, (Edward) Kamau Brathwaite, E. M. Roach, and George Lamming.

While the dominant voices in the canon had primarily been that of males, the female voice in Caribbean Poetry began to emerge with an urgent sensibility during the 1980's, the decade characterized by a burgeoning talent from the "women's quarters."[3] Some of the [then and still] most influential voices are Claire Harris, Olive Senior, Velma Pollard, M. Nourbese Philip, Pamela Mordecai, Lorna Goodison, Lillian Allen, Grace Nichols, Dionne Brand, Opal Palmer Adisa, Jean "Binta" Breeze, and Afua Cooper. Concerns surrounding sexual, social, and economic relationships that were formerly "hushed up" or rendered from male perspectives were given a new and, sometimes, initial hearing in these forceful and provocative new female voices [beginning] in the 1970's and 1980's.

Indeed, the 1980's and 1990's were bountiful periods of creativity and produced a cornucopia of talented poets. The prolific voices of this period include, but are clearly not limited to Kwame Dawes, Cyril Dabydeen, David Dabydeen, Ramabai Espinet, Ahdri Zhina Mandiela, Rachel Manley, and Sasenarine Persaud. The innovative styling of the artists working in the captivating sub-genre classified as "dub poetry" was (and continues to be) powerfully displayed in the works of Mutabaruka, Oku Onuora, Linton Kwesi Johnson, Benjamin Zephaniah, Lillian Allen, and Jean "Binta" Breeze, among others.

The proliferation of voices in the Anglophone Caribbean Poetry canon, from the late 1970's through the early 1990's, is a testament to the increase in self-publishing along with the artists' expanded access to major publishing venues. This increase in publishing activity finally afforded the poets of the Anglophone Caribbean literary tradition with a world of readers, critics, scholars, and students not only in the Caribbean but also far beyond in the various metropoles of the Caribbean Diaspora and the world at large. The poets of the Anglophone Caribbean literary tradition, indeed, were giving the scholars and critics "something to talk about."

Concurrent with the increase in published poetry, the 1970's was a period of increased literary criticism toward the construction of tenuously grounded critical and aesthetic theories on the poetry of Anglophone Caribbean writers. Critics were moving, and continue to move, beyond a type of staid theorizing toward inaugural approaches. Such approaches indicate a movement toward critiquing the poetry on "new" terms, its own terms, with language, criteria, and terminology designed to fit the differences inherent in the poetry while accommodating elements of "sameness" in the poets' extraction from the tenets and styles of the [predominantly British] literary tradition of the past.

With the recent close of the 20th century and the inauguration of the 21st century, the Anglophone Caribbean Poetry canon has grown to include an array of new works by well-known writers such as Kamau Brathwaite, Derek Walcott, Kwame Dawes, Claire Harris, and M. Nourbese Philip, among others. New voices are also emerging in the canon with an array of styles and approaches to previously treated and new subjects. Clearly, the canon is a growing, expanding, and evolving one, as this text, *Anglophone Caribbean Poetry, 1970-2001: An Annotated Bibliography*, will illustrate.

I invite you, now, to read, research, and respond to the listed works that form a large and significant portion of the Anglophone Caribbean Poetry canon.

---

[1] Brown, Stewart and John Wickham, eds. *The Oxford Book of Caribbean Short Stories*. Oxford University Press, 1999.

[2] Some of the papers presented at this conference are available at the Institute of Jamaica. The Radio Education Unit at the University of the West Indies (Mona Campus) also lists recordings of all the conference sessions in their database; however, neither tapes nor transcripts were physically available at this writing. A compilation by C. D. Narasimhaiah entitled "A. C. L. A. L. S. Conference on Commonwealth Literature: Kingston, Jamaica, January 3-9, 1971" in the *Journal of Commonwealth Literature* 6.2 (Dec. 1971): 120-26, is the most readily accessible source of information on the conference.

[3] The use of the phrase "women's quarters" alludes to the collection of poetry by Claire Harris, *Fables From the Women's Quarters* (Toronto: Williams-Wallace, 1984).

Selected Timeline of Anglophone Caribbean Poetry

1759	The first known poem published by a free Jamaican black, Francis Williams – "Ode to Governor Haldane"
1764	"Sugar Cane" published by James Grainger, British doctor on a tour of duty in Jamaica
1808	Abolition of slave trade by USA and Britain
1833	"Barbados," a poem by pro-slavery Barbadian planter M.J. Chapman, published
1838	Complete abolition of slavery in the British colonies
1841-1867	Indentured laborers arrive in the British West Indies from West Africa
1845	East Indian indentured laborers arrive in Trinidad
1869	*The Theory and Practice of Creole Grammar* written by J.J. Thomas
1883	Egbert Martin, first major poet in British Guiana, writes *Leo's Poetical Works*
1912	Claude McKay writes *Songs of Jamaica* and *Constab Ballads* – first major collection of Anglophone poems written in Creole dialect

1917   End of East Indian indenture

1919   Onset of racial protests in the United States
Claude McKay's "protest" poetry earns him renown as a major voice in the Harlem Renaissance

1922   The Jamaican Marcus Garvey forms the Universal Negro Improvement Association (UNIA) in Harlem and leads the Back-to-Africa Movement.

1923   Founding of the Jamaican Poetry League by John E. C. McFarlane and others

1929   First major anthology of Jamaican poetry, *Voices from Summerland*

1930   Una Marson publishes *Tropic Reveries,* first noted collection of poems by a West Indian woman

1931   First major anthology of poetry in [then] British Guiana, *Guianese Poetry, 1831-1931*, edited by Norman E. Cameron
Publication of the *Beacon* magazine in Trinidad

1934   Publication of the *West Indian Review*

1942   Publication of the magazine, *Bim*, in Barbados
BBC "Caribbean Voices" program begins
Publication of Louise Bennett's *Dialect Verses*

1943   Publication of *Focus* magazine in Jamaica

1945   Publication of *Kyk-over-al* magazine in Guyana
Publication of George Campbell's *First Poems*

1948   Death of Claude McKay
Founding of the University of the West Indies
[Private] publication of Walcott's *25 Poems*

1949   *Caribbean Quarterly* published at the University of the West Indies

1950   Migration of West Indians to England in large numbers
Pioneer Press in Jamaica begins operation
Derek and Roderick Walcott establish the St. Lucia Arts Guild

1951   Miniature Poets Series inaugurated by Arthur J. (A.J.) Seymour

1952   "The Glossary of Barbadian Dialect" by Frank Collymore appears in *Bim*

1954   Martin Carter, *Poems of Resistance*
Wilson Harris, *Eternity to Season*

1956   Trinidad places Eric Williams in control of the government

1958   Final broadcast of the BBC " Caribbean Voices" Program
Federation of the West Indies established (ended in 1962)

1959   Frank Collymore's *Collected Poems* published
Walcott establishes the group later known as the Trinidad Theatre Workshop

1961   *Kyk-over-al* journal ceases publication
Frederick Cassidy's *Jamaica Talk: Three Hundred Years of the English Language in Jamaica* published

1962   Jamaica and Trinidad and Tobago gain independence
West Indian immigration to Britain restricted
Walcott publishes *In A Green Night*

1963   University of Guyana is established

1965   Malcolm X assassinated in the USA
Walcott publishes *The Castaway*

1966   Barbados and Guyana gain independence
Louise Bennett publishes *Jamaica Labrish*
Caribbean Artists Movement (CAM) founded in London

1967   Brathwaite publishes *Rights of Passage*, the first part of his trilogy *The Arrivants* (followed by *Masks* in 1968 and *Islands* in 1969)
Cassidy and LePage publish *Dictionary of Jamaican English*

1968   Martin Luther King, Jr. and Robert Kennedy assassinated in the USA
Walter Rodney, Guyanese scholar, ejected from Jamaica followed by student occupation of the Creative Arts Centre at the University of the West Indies in Mona

1969   The Black Power Movement in the USA makes an impact on the literature and politics of the West Indies
Walcott publishes *The Gulf*

1970   Abortive "February Revolution" in Trinidad
First issue of *Trinidad & Tobago Review* (then *Tapia)*

1971   ACLALS Conference in Jamaica
"New Writing 1970" published in *Savacou* ¾

1972   First Caribbean Festival of the Arts (Carifesta)
Wayne Brown publishes *On the Coast*
Anthony McNeill publishes *Reel from "The Life Movie"*

1973   Dennis Scott publishes *Uncle Time*
Mervyn Morris publishes *The Pond*
Walcott publishes *Another Life*

1974   Eric Roach commits suicide
Brathwaite publishes *Dream Stories*

1977   Brathwaite publishes *Mother Poem*
Martin Carter publishes *Poems of Succession*
Oku Onuoka publishes *Echo*

1980   Walter Rodney assassinated in Guyana
A. J. Seymour publishes *A Treasury of Guyanese Poetry* (anthology)
Jamaica Woman anthology published
Goodison publishes *Tamarind Season*
Mutabaruka publishes *The First Poems: 1970-1979*

1981   Death of Bob Marley
Walcott starts teaching at Boston University
Gordon Rohlehr publishes *Pathfinder: Black Awakening in The Arrivants of Edward Kamau Brathwaite*

1982   Brathwaite publishes *Sun Poem*
Dennis Scott publishes *Dreadwalk*

1983   Mikey Smith stoned to death in Kingston, Jamaica
M. Nourbese Philip publishes *Salmon Courage*

1984   Grace Nichols publishes *Fat Black Woman's Poems*
              David Dabydeen publishes *Slave Song*
              Lloyd Brown publishes *West Indian Poetry* (2nd edition, Heinemann)

1986   Walcott publishes *Collected Poems*
              Paula Burnett publishes *Penguin Book of Caribbean Verse*

1987   Brathwaite publishes *X/Self*
              Brathwaite wins Commonwealth Prize for Poetry

1988   Death of Martin Carter
              First International Congress of Caribbean Women Writers held
              at Wellesley College
              Frank Birbalsingh publishes *Jahaji Bhai: An Anthology of
              Indo-Caribbean Literature*

1990   Walcott publishes *Omeros*
              Ramabai Espinet publishes *Creation Fire: A CAFRA Anthology of
              Caribbean Women's Poetry*

1991   Brathwaite starts teaching at New York University

1992   Nobel Prize for Literature awarded to Walcott
              Anne Walmsley publishes *The Caribbean Artists Movement 1966-
              1972: A Literary and Cultural History*

1993   J. Edward Chamberlin publishes *Come Back To Me My Language:
              Poetry and the West Indies*

1994   Brathwaite wins Neustadt International Prize for Literature

1995   Bruce King publishes *West Indian Literature* (2nd edition)

1996   International Conference of Caribbean Women Writers and
              Scholars held at Florida International University

1998   First Annual International Conference on Caribbean Literature
              (ICCL) held in the Bahamas
              Laurence Breiner publishes *An Introduction to West Indian Poetry*

2000   Claire Harris publishes *She,* her seventh volume of poetry
              Brathwaite publishes *Words Need Love Too*

2001   Pamela Mordecai publishes volume of poems, *Certifiable*
Fourth Annual International Conference on Caribbean Literature
(ICCL) held in Martinique
Brathwaite publishes *Ancestors*

I.   *Anthologies*

001.   Agard, John and Grace Nichols, eds. *A Caribbean Dozen.* MA: Candlewick Press, 1994.

This collection of works by thirteen Caribbean poets is largely directed toward young children; however, adult readers will get an indication of the writers' artistry from the selections. Poetry by Valerie Bloom, Faustin Charles, Grace Nichols, Telcine Turner, David Campbell, Opal Palmer Adisa, Marc Matthews, John Agard, Dionne Brand, Pamela Mordecai, John Lyons, James Berry, and Frank Collymore are included. The text is illustrated by Cathie Felstead.

002.   Allis, Jeanette B. and Latifah Lois Chinnery, eds. *Proud of Our Land and People: A Virgin Islands Poetry Collection.* Charlotte Amalie, USVI: Bureau of Libraries, Museums and Archeological Services, 1984.

The poems in this collection were selected from submissions to the Enid M. Baa Library and Archives for a poetry contest under the sponsorship of the Friends of the Baa Library and the Virgin Islands Council on the Arts.   Poems are written by children and adults.   The collection also contains photographs and children's sketches.

003.   Bensen, Robert, ed. *One People's Grief: Recent Writings from the Caribbean.* Hamilton, N.Z.: Outrigger Publishers, 1983.

This collection gathers the work of writers in the English-speaking Caribbean (Derek Walcott, Jean Rhys, Kamau Brathwaite, Bruce St. John, Timothy Callendar, O. R. Dathorne, Austin Clarke, Howard A. Fergus, Ann Marie Dewar, Sidney Collie, Edward Baugh, Lorna Goodison, Andrew Salkey, E. O. Ledgister, Cyril Dabydeen, et. al.), alongside the work of the French-speaking writers Aime Cesaire and Paul Larague and ten poets of the Cuban Revolution (Alejo Carpentier, Nicolas Guillen, et. al.).

004.   Berry, James, ed. *Bluefoot Traveller: Poetry by Westindians in Britain.* Rev. ed. London: Harrap, 1985.

An anthology of the work of West Indian poets living in Britain. Contains the work of eleven poets for a total of 38 poems. Readers are made aware of the central concerns of West Indians living in Britain.

005.   _____, ed. *News for Babylon: The Chatto Book of Westindian-British Poetry.* London: Chatto and Windus, 1984.

This anthology expands upon the work started in Berry's *Bluefoot Traveller.* It contains the work of 40 poets for a total of 154 poems. All included poets live in Britain or have previously lived in Britain. Poets such as Linton Kwesi Johnson, Benjamin Zephaniah, Faustin Charles, Vivian Usherwood, Valerie Bloom, John Agard, and Grace Nichols are featured.

006.   Birbalsingh, Frank, ed. *Jahaji Bhai: An Anthology of Indo-Caribbean Literature.* Toronto: TSAR, 1988.

The title of this anthology "Jahaji Bhai" is a Hindi expression which means "ship brother." The writing of descendants of Indian indenture in the Caribbean appears in this collection. Included are seven short stories, three nonfiction works, one folktale in Guyanese dialect, and poems by Rajumarie Singh, Ramabai Espinet, Mahadai Das, Alim Mohamed, Arnold Itwaru, and Cyril Dabydeen.

007.   Brathwaite, Edward Kamau, ed. *Dream Rock* (with an introduction by Winnie Risden-Hunter). Kingston, Jamaica: Jamaica Information Service, 1987.

This is a collection of poems which, according to the editor (Brathwaite), reflects the thought and style of some of the younger, promising poets in their depiction of issues of home, country, and identity. Poets included are Jean L. Goulbourne, Hall Anthony Ellis, Pam Gordon Hickling, Mark Lee, Roy Thomas, Brenda E. Campbell, Elaine Thompson, and Janneth Morgan.

008.   _____, ed. *New Poets from Jamaica: An Anthology*. Kingston, Jamaica: Savacou, 1979.

Brathwaite presents this anthology and its poets as heralders of the third revolution of Caribbean poetry in English. The works of Pam Hickling, Pam Mordecai, Christine Craig, Jean Goulbourne, Opal Palmer, Brian Meeks, Oku Onuora, Michael Smith, Noel Walcott, Lorna Goodison, Bob Stewart, Beverly Brown, and Lloyd Richardson are featured.

009.   Brown, Stewart, ed. *Caribbean New Voices*. Vol. 1. Harlow, England: Longman Caribbean, 1995.

This is a diverse collection of poems and stories by Caribbean writers, particularly new writers. All writers in this collection have published some work in the Caribbean. The poetry in this collection represents the stylistic range of the genre. Notable are the poems of Howard A. Fergus, Michael Gilkes, Judith Hamilton, Al Creighton, and Patricia Turnball.

010.   _____, ed. *Caribbean Poetry Now*. 2nd ed. London: Edward Arnold, 1992.

This anthology contains a foreword by poet and critic Mervyn Morris. An introduction written by Stewart Brown (editor) follows. The text has been designed to assist students prepare for the CXC English B Examination. Divided into the following sections: Roots, Childhood and Adolescence; Folks; One Love; Home-City Life; Home-Country Life; Old Folks, Death, and Grief; and Gods, Ghosts, and Spirits.

011.   Brown, Stewart, Mervyn Morris, and Gordon Rohlehr, eds. *Voiceprint: An Anthology of Oral and Related Poetry from the Caribbean*. Longmann Caribbean, 1989.

An introduction by Gordon Rohlehr is followed by a large number of poems under the following thematic/descriptive headings: Legend, Tale, Narrative, and Folk-song, Elegy and Lament, Dreadtalk, Dub, Sermon, Prophesight and Prophesay, Calypso, Pan, Calypso, and Rapso Poems, Parang and Hosay, Monologues, Signifying, Robber Talk, Praise Songs, Prayers and Incantations, Tracing, Curses and Other Warnings, Political Manifestoes and Satire, Voice Portraits, and Word-Songs.

012.   Burnett, Paula, ed. *The Penguin Book of Caribbean Verse in English*. London: Penguin Books Ltd., 1986.

Published in 1986, this is still a very important and reliable anthology of Anglophone Caribbean poetry. It is organized into two major sections:

the oral tradition and the literary tradition. The introduction and the biographical and explanatory notes serve as a reference for researchers and students wanting to become familiar with the scope of Anglophone Caribbean poetry.

013.   Cameron, Norman Eustace, ed. *Guianese Poetry: Covering the Hundred Years' Period, 1831-1931*. Nendeln, Liechtenstein: Kraus Reprint, 1970.

First published in the 1930s, this text compiles select poetry of a hundred year period. The text is divided into four sections: Narrative Poems, Topical and Miscellaneous Poems, Moral and Religious Poems, and Concluding Poems.

014.   Campbell, Marty, ed. *Collage Two: Poems by Poets of St. Croix*. Christiansted, St. Croix, USVI: Antilles Press, 1991.

This collection follows *Collage One* which was edited by Campbell's colleague, Arnold Highfield. These poems grew out of the informal poetry readings at Collage Café in St. Croix. Contains the work of twenty poets and includes a glossary of terms.

015.   Clarke, Sebastian. *New Planet: Anthology of Modern Caribbean Writing*. London: Karnak House, 1978.

This anthology places emphasis on how Caribbean writers express world power and the concept of minorities. Clarke contends that the offerings in this anthology represent the establishment of unique writing models. Works by John La Rose, Mervyn Taylor, George Calhoun, and others are included.

016.   Cooper, Afua, ed. *Utterance and Incantations: Women, Poetry, and Dub*. Toronto: Sister Vision Press, 1999.

The works of eleven female dub poets – Lillian Allen, amuna barak, Michelle Barrow, Louise Bennett, Jean Breeze, Afua Cooper, Queen Majeeda, Cherry Natural, ahdri zhina mandiela, Deanne Smith, and Anita Stewart aka Anilia Soyinka - are collected by Afua Cooper in this, the first, anthology of dub poetry by women. The introduction contains a brief yet clear historical background of dub poetry and the female impact on the genre. Photographs of the poets precede their work.

017.   Dabydeen, Cyril, ed. *A Shapely Fire: Changing the Literary Landscape*. Oakville: Mosaic Press, 1987.

This anthology contains the work of twenty writers born in the Caribbean who currently reside [or have formerly resided] in Canada. Prose and drama are included alongside poetry by Claire Harris, Daniel Caudeiron, Marlene Nourbese Philip, Cyril Dabydeen, Abdur-Rahman Slade Hopkinson, Lillian Allen, Horace Goddard, Charles Roach, Dionne Brand, Arnold Itwaru, Edward Watson, Karl Gordon, and Anthony Phelps.

018.   Dathorne, O. R., ed. *Caribbean Verse*. London: Heinemann, 1980.

In the introduction, Dathorne contends that the selected poems reflect the domestic origins of the poets. Emphasis is placed on the historical backgrounds and traditions of West Indian Poetry. The work of twenty-seven poets are featured.

019.   Dawes, Kwame, ed. *Wheel and Come Again: An Anthology of Reggae Poetry*. Fredericton, N.B. : Goose Lane, 1997.

This anthology gathers the work of poets who use nation language, Rasta-speech, and Rasta invention with the flavor of reggae. The works of thirty-nine poets are included.

020.   Dawes, Neville and Anthony McNeill, eds. *The Caribbean Poem: An Anthology of Fifty Caribbean Voices*. [s. l.] Carifesta 76, 1976.

This publication collects poems from the 1976 Carifesta (Caribbean Festival of the Arts). Carifesta 1976 was held in Jamaica. It was the second of the Carifesta events which continue into the present.

021.   Donnell, Alison and Sarah Lawson Welsh, eds. *The Routledge Reader in Caribbean Literature*. New York: Routledge, 1996.

This reader provides a historical and cultural foundation to the student of Caribbean literature, culturally and aesthetically, from 1900 through the 1990's. The reader contains poetry, short stories, essays, articles, and interviews.

022.   Drayton, Arthur, ed. *Caribanthology 2: On Justice – Human Rights*. Barbados: The Cedar Press, 1981.

This anthology collects poems that deal with the denial of justice and human rights to (African) Caribbeans. The poems also reflect the poets' movement towards language that portrays an indigenous voice. Poets such as Mervyn Morris, Oku Onuora, Kendel Hippolyte, Pamela Mordecai, Howard Fergus, Lorna Goodison, and Mutabaruka are featured.

023.   Espinet, Ramabai, ed. *Creation Fire: A CAFRA Anthology of Caribbean Women's Poetry.* Toronto: Sister Vision Press, 1990.

The concept for this anthology came out of the beginnings of CAFRA (Caribbean Association for Feminine Research and Action) in 1985. An introduction by Espinet provides information on background, selection, themes, contributors, and poetic voices in the collection. Includes poems in English, Spanish, Dutch and French; poems in Spanish, Dutch, and French are accompanied by translations in English.

024.   Fenwick, M. J., ed. *Sisters of Caliban - Contemporary Women Poets of the Caribbean: A Multi-Lingual Anthology.* Falls Church, VA: Azul Press, 1996.

A multilingual anthology of Caribbean women poets, the thematic emphasis is a defiant protest of past and continuing colonial philosophies, practices, and policies. Contains biographical notes.

025.   Fergus, Howard A. and Larry Rowdon, eds. *Dark Against the Sky: An Anthology of Poems and Short Stories From Montserrat.* Plymouth, Montserrat: University of the West Indies School of Continuing Studies, 1990.

This anthology contains the work of 27 writers of poetry and short stories. The poems focus on local life and experience in Montserrat, as well as world issues from a Caribbean perspective.

026.   _____, ed. *Flowers Blooming Late: Poems From Montserrat.* Plymouth, Montserrat: University Centre, University of the West Indies, 1984.

This anthology commemorates the emancipation of slaves. Works are written by Montserratians at home and abroad. Also includes works by new residents to the island.

027.   _____, ed.. *Horrors of a Hurricane: Poems.* Plymouth, Montserrat: School of Continuing Studies, University of the West Indies, 1990.

This is an anthology of poetry written by people of Montserrat from all walks of life. The 31 poems deal with the devastation of Montserrat after Hurricane Hugo, believed to be their worst hurricane to date.

028.   Figueredo, Alfred E., ed. *Collage Three: Poems of St. Croix.* Christiansted, St. Croix, USVI: Antilles Press, 1993.

This is the third poetry annual published by poets who met regularly at the Café Collage in St. Croix. These annuals represent the collective work of the first literary movement in St. Croix. Contains the work of fifteen poets.

029.   Figueroa, John, ed. *Caribbean Voices: An Anthology of West Indian Poetry.* 2nd ed. London: Evans Brothers, 1982.

Second edition of the anthology originally published in 1966. The poems are presented in six sections: People, Nature, Art, In Our Land, Interlude, and Beyond. Suggestions for further reading are given at the end of the text.

030.   Forde, Alfred Nathaniel, ed. *Talk of the Tamarinds: An Anthology of Poetry.* London: E. Arnold Publishers Ltd., 1971.

In a brief introduction, Forde discusses the art of creating poetry. The collection of poems, many written by people born in the Caribbean, is divided into eight sections: The Sea and Ships; Doing Things, Shaping Life; People and Home; The Lighter Side of Life; Nature, the Giver, the Teacher; Coming Up Against Life; Birds, Animals, and Us; and Looking Back.

031.   Giuseppe, Neville and Undine Giuseppe, eds. *Out for Stars: An Anthology of Poetry.* London: Macmillan, 1975-1976. 2 vols.

This anthology is unique in that the poets come from many countries such as the Caribbean, United States of America, Africa, China, India, and the United Kingdom. Some of the included West Indian poets appear in print for the first time. The anthology is divided into five sections: People, Places, Things Seen and Heard, Ballads and Narrative Verse, and Reflective and Nostalgic Poems.

032.   Gonzalez, Anson and Kenneth Vidia Parmasad, eds. *Arising: Writers Union of Trinidad & Tobago Fifth Anniversary Anthology.* Trinidad/ Tobago: Writers Union of Trinidad and Tobago, 1985.

This anthology of poetry commemorates the fifth anniversary of the Writers Union of Trinidad and Tobago. Contains poems by new and well-known writers such as James C. Aboud, Marina Omowale Maxwell, Anson Gonzalez, Paul Keens Douglas, Victor D. Questel, Pearl Eintou Springer, K. V. Parmasad, and O. Babatunde.

033.   Habekost, Christian, ed. *Dub Poetry: 19 Poets from England and Jamaica.* Germany: Michael Schwinn, 1987.

This is the first full length discussion of dub poetry accompanied by select poems from 19 poets classified as "dub" artists. Section I contains a background of Dub Poetry divided into five sections: Word, Sound & Power; In the Beginning Was the Word …and the rhythm; The Sound of Drum, Bass, and Voice; The Oral Tradition; and The Power: Poetry as Performance. Part II contains the work of 19 dub poets form England and Jamaica

034.   Harris, Claire and Edna Alford, eds. *Kitchen Talk: Contemporary Women's Prose and Poetry.* Red Deer College Press, 1992.

Harris and Alford use the kitchen as the focal point of creativity of the included poetry, prose, interviews, and oral transcriptions of Canadian women. Some West Indian Canadian women writers are featured (e.g. Nourbese Philip, et.al.)

035.   Hearne, John, ed. *Carifesta Forum: An Anthology of 20 Caribbean Voices.* Kingston, Jamaica: Institute of Jamaica and Jamaica Journal, 1976.

In preparing this anthology for the 1976 CARIFESTA, Hearne suggested the theme should be a definition of the present state of culture in the Caribbean during a "turbulent, complicated and often painful time of transition." Works from writers of varied styles are included: C.L.R. James, Aime Cesaire, George Lamming, Derek Walcott, Kamau Brathwaite, Wilson Harris, and others. An introduction is written by Hearne.

036.   Highfield, Arnold, ed. *Collage One: Poems by Poets of St. Croix.* Christiansted, St. Croix, U.S.V.I.: Antilles Press, 1990.

This book of poetry was produced after Hurricane Hugo swept through St. Croix, V.I. While this collection grew out of emotions following the hurricane, only a few poems deal with the storm directly. Poems are written by Marty Campbell, Alfredo E. Figueredo, Gary Harold, Arnold R. Highfield, S.B. Jones-Hendrickson, Richard Schrader, Erika Smilowitz, Guy Stiles, and Mark Sylvester.

037.   Hill, Valdemar A., ed. *Sun Island Jewels: An Anthology of Virgin Islands Poetry.* Charlotte Amalie, USVI: Val Hill Enterprises, 1975.

This collection of poems reflects a wide range of self-expression within the Virgin Islands through varied poetic styles. Poets from St. Thomas, St. Croix, St. John, and Virgin Gorda are featured.

038. Hippolyte, Kendel, ed. *Confluence: Nine St. Lucian Poets.* Castries, St. Lucia: The Source, 1988.

The preface written by Hippolyte places emphasis on the diversity of the poetry in the anthology in terms of ideas, sounds, images, and rhythms. Work from McDonald Dixon, John Robert Lee, Kendel Hippolyte, Jane King, Irvin Desir, Egbert Lucien, Melchoir Henry, Adrian Augier, and Melania Daniel.

039. _____, ed. *So Much Poetry in We People: An Anthology of Performance Poetry.* [s. l.] Eastern Caribbean Popular Theatre Organisation, 1990.

This collection of performance poems by thirteen poets is preceded by a Foreword written by Kendel Hippolyte. In the Foreword, he offers a definition of perfomance poetry and its overall purposes and impact on audiences. Poems are grouped in four thematic sections: History and Political Action, Living in the System, Culture – Celebration and Warning, and Woman.

040. Jones, Esmor, ed. *Heritage: A Caribbean Anthology.* London: Cassell Ltd., 1981.

This text, a combination of poems, short stories, and passages, is written primarily by Caribbean authors. The book has been designed to assist Caribbean students prepare for the Secondary Education Certificate in English. Divided into sections: Places, People and Families, Work and Leisure, In A Strange Land, and Inheritance.

041. Jones-Hendrickson, Simon B., ed. *Of Masks and Mysteries: Poems.* Frederiksted, VI: Eastern Caribbean Institute, 1993.

This anthology contains poems by Michael H. Lythoe, Vincent O. Cooper, Earthla Arthur, Simon B. Jones-Hendrickson, Lillian Sutherland, and Regina Joseph.

042. Kellman, Tony, ed. *Crossing Water: Contemporary Poetry of the English-Speaking Caribbean.* NY: Greenfield Review Press, 1992.

This anthology reflects the multiple voices and cultures of the Caribbean region. Issues of survival and identity emerge in the poems of 37 writers. An introduction by Kellman presents an overview of the evolution of Caribbean poetry since the early 1930s.

043.   Krise, Thomas W., ed. _Caribbeana: An Anthology of English Literature of the West Indies, 1657-1777_. Chicago: University of Chicago Press, 1999.

Krise contends that the aim of this text is to illuminate the role of the West Indies in the English-speaking culture. The works included in this anthology are representative samples of published writing on the British West Indies between the Protectorship of Oliver Cromwell and the beginning of the American Revolution. Early poetry by James Grainger and Francis Williams is included.

044.   Kwashi, Nii, ed. _Rampart II: As We Ponder – Poems_. Roseau, Dominica: Frontline Co-operative, 1988.

This is the second collection of poems by the members of the Frontline Cooperative. The poems focus on memories of friends and past times. Poets included are Ras Moses, Gabriel Christian, Christabel La Ronde, Eddie 'Izar' Toulon, Steve 'Nii Kwashi' Roberts, Frank Jno. Baptiste, and Dawen Daway. Brief biographies of the poets are included.

045.   Lewis, Maureen Warner, ed. _Yoruba Songs of Trinidad with Translations_. London: Karnak House, 1994.

This is the first published collection of Yoruba poems, folksongs, and sacred chants from Trinidad. The formulaic structures of the songs and poems (treated as a body of oral literature) are explained in footnotes.

046.   Lightbourne, Ronald, ed. _This Is My Country: Prize Winning Poetry from Bermuda_. Southhampton, Bermuda: Bermuda for Bermudians, 1978.

This collection of poems grew out of the 1977 Poetry Contest of Bermuda For Bermudians. The winning entries comprise this text. The poetry of novice and more seasoned writers is included.

047.   Livingston, James T., ed. _Caribbean Rhythms: The Emerging English Literature of the West Indies_. New York: Washington Square Press, 1974.

This anthology contains short stories, poems, essays, and dramatic works. The poetry section is representative of the major poets in the English-speaking Caribbean with an emphasis on Jamaican poets.

048.   Malik, Abdul, ed. _De Homeplace: Poems for Renewal by Young People of Caribbean Origin_. London: Panrun Collective, 1990.

This anthology consists of previously unpublished poems written by 25 year olds and under living in the Caribbean and/or [of Caribbean descent] Britain, Germany, Canada, and North America. The poems deal with issues of identity, transmigration, sexual conflict, and love.

049.   Markham, E. A., ed. *Hinterland: Caribbean Poetry from the West Indies & Britain*. London: Bloodaxe Books, 1989.

This anthology begins with a lengthy introduction by Markham which justifies purpose, organization, and title of the text. Selected poems, essays, and interviews with fourteen Caribbean poets – Louise Bennett, Martin Carter, Derek Walcott, Kamau Brathwaite, Dennis Scott, Mervyn Morris, James Berry, E.A. Markham, Olive Senior, Lorna Goodison, Linton Kwesi Johnson, Michael Smith, Grace Nichols, and Fred D'Aguiar - are included.

050.   McDonald, Ian and Stewart Brown, eds. *The Heinemann Book of Caribbean Poetry*. Heinemann, 1992.

The editors contend, in the introduction, that West Indian poetry is one of the "real" growing areas of contemporary literature. The editors have included established as well as new poets, avoiding the inclusion of standard anthology selections. Biographical notes follow and conclude the anthology.

051.   Mordecai, Pamela, ed. *From Our Yard: Jamaican Poetry Since Independence – The First Twenty-Five Years*. Rev. ed. Jamaica 21 Anthology Series. Institute of Jamaica Publications Ltd., 1991.

A collection of poems by some of the most well-known voices of the post-independence era. Works are included from poets in Jamaica as well as those abroad who maintain a central concern and affinity for their homes. Includes biographical notes.

052.   Mordecai, Pamela and Grace Walker Gordon, eds. *Sunsong 2*. Longman Group UK Limited, 1992.

This anthology contains poems by authors from the Caribbean and other parts of the world. A short biography is provided for each poet along with questions on each poem. *Sunsong* is designed to teach students how to interpret poems during their first three years of secondary school.

053.   _____, eds. *Sunsong 3*. Longman Group UK Limited, 1992.

This anthology follows the structure of *Sunsong 2*. Contains questions and notes for all poems.

054.   _____, eds. *Sunsong Tide Rising: Anthology*. San Juan, Trinidad: Longman Caribbean, 1994.

This anthology continues the focus of *Sunsong 1, 2*, and *3* and is a showcase of poetry from the Caribbean as well as other areas of the world. Divided into eleven thematic sections.

055.   Mordecai, Pamela and Mervyn Morris, eds. *Jamaica Woman: An Anthology of Poems*. Kingston: Heinemann, 1980.

At the time of this publication each of the female poets had yet to publish a separate volume of her poems. The anthology features the works of Jennifer Brown, Christine Craig, Jean D'Costa, Dorothea Edmondson, Lorna Goodison, Sally Henzell, Bridget Jones, Sandy McIntosh, Alma MockYen, Velma Pollard, Heather Royes, Olive Senior, Colleen Smith-Brown, Cyrene Tomlinson, and Pamela Mordecai. Biographical notes are included.

056.   Morris, Mervyn, ed. *Focus 1983: An Anthology of Contemporary Jamaican Writing*. Kingston, Jamaica: Caribbean Authors Publishing Co., Ltd., 1983.

This compilation of previously unpublished prose fiction and poetry was an effort to revive the journal *Focus* which was originally published by Edna Manley in 1943, 1948, 1956, and 1960. Lorna Goodison and Edward Baugh worked with Morris on the selection of works for this issue of *Focus*.

057.   _____, ed. *Seven Jamaican Poets: An Anthology of Recent Poetry*. Jamaica: Bolivar Press, 1971.

An anthology of poems by seven Jamaica writers: A. L. Hendricks, Basil McFarlane, R.L.C. McFarlane, Edward Baugh, Mervyn Morris, Dennis Scott, and Anthony McNeill. All of these poets have published poems in Caribbean newspapers, magazines, or journals.

058.   Nettleford, Rex and Marcella Taylor, eds. *Bahamian Anthology*. London: Macmillan Caribbean, 1983.

This is the first anthology of Bahamian literature – prose, poetry, and plays. A foreword is written by Rex Nettleford and a critical introduction by Marcella Taylor.

059. Pollard, Velma, ed. *Nine West Indian Poets: An Anthology.* London: Collins, 1980.

This collection of poems is structured to prepare students for the CXC exams in English. Works by the following poets are included: Edward Brathwaite, Wayne Brown, Martin Carter, Frank Collymore, Mervyn Morris, E. M. Roach, Dennis Scott, A. J. Seymour, and Derek Walcott.

060. Ramchand, Kenneth and Cecil Gray, eds. *West Indian Poetry: An Anthology for Schools.* 2nd rev. ed. Longman Caribbean, 1989.

In the introduction of this anthology Ramchand clearly states that the text's arrangement along thematic lines with discussion topics is primarily for young people preparing for the CXC examination. Poems from major Caribbean poets up to the late 1980's are grouped according to the following themes: This Land, Struggle and Endurance, Growing Up, Encounters, Men and Women, Being A Woman, Politics and Society, Creators, Dilemmas, and Time, Folkways, Religion.

061. Salkey, Andrew, ed. *Breaklight: The Poetry of the Caribbean.* Garden City, NY: Doubleday, 1973.

This is a collection of the works of more than forty modern Caribbean poets. This volume was first published in London under the title *Breaklight: An Anthology of Caribbean Poetry.*

062. Sander, Reinhard W., ed. *From Trinidad: An Anthology of Early West Indian Writing.* London: Hodder and Stoughton, 1978.

This collection of works stems from the early material produced largely in the Trinidad magazines, *Trinidad* and *The Beacon.* Sander contends that the works are assembled to allow for a fresh examination of early West Indian writing. The anthology is divided into four sections: Literature and Culture, Short Fiction, Poetry, and Articles.

063. Seymour, Arthur J., ed. *A Treasury of Guyanese Poetry.* Georgetown: Guyana National Lithographic, 1980.

This anthology collects the poetry written in Guyana for a 150 year period (1831-1980). The period has been roughly divided into two periods (1830-1940 and 1940-80) by the following sections: People, Love, Children, Nature, Landscape, Historical, Protest, Elegies, Philosophy, Religion, and Narrative.

064.   Seymour, Elma, ed. *Sun Is A Shapely Fire: Fifty Guyanese Poems.* Georgetown: Labour Advocate, 1973.

A foreword by Lucille E. Campbell and an introduction by Elma Seymour explain that this anthology was designed as a contribution to International Book Year 1972 for the benefit of the secondary school population. The majority of these poems are written by Guyanese citizens [with a few exceptions]. The poems are organized in sections: Place Poems, Nature Poems, Seasons, People, Birds of Guyana and the Manatee, and Guyana Flora.

065.   Seymour, Stanley, ed. *Bermuda Folklore and Calypso Poems.* London: Avon, 1995.

This three time Bermuda Calypso King has assembled a collection of folklore and calypso poems germane to Bermuda. Seymour includes a brief definition of folklore and folk at the beginning of the text.

066.   Watts, Margaret, ed. *Washer Woman Hangs Her Poems in the Sun: Poems by Women of Trinidad and Tobago.* Trinidad: Gloria Ferguson Ltd., 1990.

This is the first anthology of poems by women of Trinidad and Tobago. Of the twenty-four poets featured, only three have had volumes of their poetry published. The poems are grouped in sections: dance like literature, heart ... pure an clean an happy, cloud an bamboo an bird, tongue-speak out, man crab, plenty hardship ... trouble, too, and plenty love.

067.   Wilson, Donald G., ed. *New Ships: An Anthology of West Indian Poems for Secondary Schools.* London: Oxford University Press, 1975.

This anthology of West Indian poetry was designed for use in the 7th, 8th, and 9th grades of Jamaican Secondary Schools [and contains a majority of Jamaican poems]. A foreword written by Edward Baugh, Jamaican poet and critic, explains the intent of the compilers of this anthology. The text is organized into sections: Poems for Grade 7, Poems for Grade 8, and Poems for Grade 9.

II. *References: Bibliographies, Dictionaries, and Indexes*

068.   Allis, Jeanette B, ed. *West Indian Literature: An Index to Criticism, 1930-1975.* Boston: G.K. Hall, 1981.

This compilation is arranged in three sections: 1) Index of Authors, 2) Index of Critics and Reviewers, and 3) Index of General Articles. This listing of over 2,000 articles also includes listings of reviews of novels, poetry, and collections of short stories.

069.   Allsopp, Richard, ed. *Dictionary of Caribbean English Usage.* Oxford University Press, 1996.

This dictionary expands the focus of Casssidy and LePage's *Dictionary of Jamaican English* (1967, 1st ed. and 1980, 2nd ed.) and Holm and Shillings' *Dictionary of Bahamian English* (1982) by presenting a "complete" inventory of the language of the English-speaking Caribbean territories. Definitions of words, their origins, and pronunciations, which are not available in British and American desk dictionaries, are the strengths of this compilation.

070.   Asein, Samuel Omo, ed. "West Indian Poetry in English 1900-1970: A Selected Bibliography." *Black Images : A Critical Quarterly on Black Arts and Culture* 1.2 (1972): 12-15.

This short bibliography is the first devoted to the poetry of the English-speaking Caribbean. The bibliography is organized into four sections: Bibliographies, Anthologies, Individual Authors, and Criticism (A. Books, Mimeographs, and Theses and B. Periodical Articles and Reviews).

071.   Benson, Eugene and L. W. Conolly, eds. *Encyclopedia of Post-Colonial Literatures in English.* Vols. 1-2. Routledge, 1994.

Contains sections on Caribbean Literature Anthologies, British Influences in Caribbean Literature, Black Writers in Britain, Children's Literature in the Caribbean, Literary Criticism in the Caribbean, and biographical sketches of some Caribbean writers.

072.   Benson, Eugene and William Toye, eds. *The Oxford Companion to Canadian Literature.* 2nd ed. Oxford University Press, 1997.

Contains a section on Caribbean-Canadian Literature in English and several biographical sketches of [some] Caribbean writers living in Canada.

073.   Berrian, Brenda F. and Aart Broek, eds. *Bibliography of Women Writers From the Caribbean.* Washington, D.C.: Three Continents Press, 1989.

This bibliography lists creative works – novels, short stories, poetry, folklore, autobiographies, biographies, and children's literature – by women writers of Caribbean Literature in English, French, Dutch, Spanish, Creole, Sranen Tongo, and Papiamento. Literary criticism, book reviews, and cook books are also included.

074.   Brathwaite, Doris Monica, ed. *A Descriptive and Chronological Bibliography of the Work of Edward Kamau Brathwaite (1950-1982).* London: New Beacon Books, 1988.

This bibliography covers the period of 1950-1982 and is organized by the following materials: Books/pamphlets and miscellaneous monographs, books and pamphlets edited or with contributions by the author, contributions to periodicals, and recordings.

075.   _____, ed. *Edward Kamau Brathwaite, His Published Prose and Poetry 1948-1986: A Checklist.* Mona: Savacou Cooperative, 1986.

This was a bibliography of Brathwaite's prose and poetry from 1948-1986 compiled by his wife as a research segment for her BA programme at UWI.

076.   Brathwaite, Edward Kamau, ed. *Barbados Poetry, 1661-1979: A Checklist: Books, Pamphlets, Broad Sheets.* Mona, Jamaica: Savacou Publications, 1979.

A listing of works by 70 poets (50 of Barbadian origin) is alphabetically organized by title and author in three period divisions. Works by non-Barbadians, such as Derek Walcott and Wilfred Cartey are included. No publication information is listed with the works.

077.   ____, ed. *Jamaica Poetry, A Checklist: Books, Pamphlets, and Sheets, 1686-1978.* Kingston: Jamaica Library Service, 1979.

Listings are by author and title. The works of about 150 Jamaicans are collected in three periods: 1) Slavery, 2) Colonial Period, and 3) 1900 – the Present. Notes on some of the poets are included. No publication information is listed with the works.

078.   Carnegie, Jeniphier R, ed. *Critics on West Indian Literature: A Selected Bibliography.* Mona, Jamaica: Research and Publications Committee, University of the West Indies, 1979.

A listing of 741 items, this text is arranged in two sections: A) Individual Authors (to include Michael Anthony, Edward Kamau Brathwaite, Theodore Wilson Harris, George Lamming, Roger Mais, Edgar Austin Mittelholzer, V.S. Naipaul, Victor Reid, Jean Rhys, Andrew Salkey, Samuel Selvon, and Derek Walcott) and B) i.) Bibliographies and Indexes and ii) Criticisms on West Indian Literature. Entries are arranged by author.

079.   ____, ed. "Select Bibliography of the Literature of the English-Speaking West Indies, 1989-1991." *Journal of West Indian Literature* 7.1 (1996): 1-53.

This bibliography is useful to students, professors, and research scholars as a checklist of work by West Indian writers, both well-known and lesser known. Poetry scholars will be particularly interested in the sections: Anthologies, Periodicals, Poetry, Juvenile Literature, Bibliographies, Criticism: General Studies.

080.   Comitas, Lambros, ed. *The Complete Caribbeana, 1900-1975: A Bibliographic Guide to the Scholarly Literature.* Millwood, NY: KTO Press, 1977.

This is a major bibliographic collection designed to enhance scholarly research on the Caribbean region. The work is divided into four volumes: 1) People, 2) Institutions, 3) Resources, and 4) Indexes. The volumes are divided into nine major thematic sections: A) Introduction to the Caribbean, B) The Past, C) The People, D) Elements of Culture, E) Health, F) Education and Welfare G) Political Issues, H) Socioeconomic Activities and Institutions, I) The Environment and Human Geography, and J) Soils, Crops, and Livestocks.

081.   Cassidy, Frederick G. and R. B. Le Page, eds. *Dictionary of Jamaican English*. 2nd ed. London: Cambridge University Press, 1980.

This is a descriptive historical dictionary of the English language in all of its forms in Jamaica. This edition updates the 1967 edition . This update includes a supplement (pp. 491-509) as well as a revision of the introductory chapters and the bibliography. Includes a linguistic introduction on the historical phonology of Jamaican English.

082.   Dance, Daryl Cumber, ed. *Fifty Caribbean Writers: A Bio-Bibliographical Critical Sourcebook*. Greenwood Press, 1986.

This text is comprised of fifty essays on a range of important Caribbean writers. Each essay contains biographical information, a critical review of the writer's major works and themes, an evaluative survey of selected scholarship, and a listing of major honors and awards. A bibliography of primary and secondary works, with publication data, concludes each essay.

083.   Fenwick, M. J., ed. *Writers of the Caribbean and Central America: A Bibliography*. Vols. 1-2. New York: Garland, 1992.

This bibliography collects the literature of authors working within the literary tradition of the Caribbean Basin Region and Central America. Writers' original works are listed, followed by magazines and anthologies in which the authors' works appear. Both recognized and new writers are featured.

084.   Fister, Barbara, ed. *Third World Women's Literatures: A Dictionary and Guide to Materials in English*. Greenwood Press, 1995.

According to the author, this is primarily a dictionary with three types of entries: biographical, individual works of literature, and thematic literary works and commentary on a broad range of issues in Third World Women's Literatures.

085.   Gonzalez, Anson, ed. *Creative Writing in the Republic of Trinidad and Tobago, 1962-1977: A Bibliography.* Trinidad, 1977.

This is a chronological listing of works by genre – novels, poems, short stories, biography, autobiography, and plays. This compilation also contains lists of journals, magazines, and yearbooks.

086.   Goslinga, Marian, ed. *Caribbean Literature: A Bibliography.* Lanham, Md. and London: Scarecrow Press, Inc., 1998.

This is the first comprehensive general bibliography on the Caribbean Basin Region since the 1977 publication of Lambros Comitas' *Complete Caribbeana.* The text is organized into three major sections: Historical Materials, Reference and Source Materials, and Contemporary Works.

087.   Hamilton, Ian, ed. *The Oxford Companion to Twentieth Century Poetry in English.* Oxford University Press, 1994.

This compilation contains biographical sketches of some Caribbean writers of 20th century poetry (written in English) as well as those of poets of other backgrounds writing in English.

088.   Herdeck, Donald E., ed. *Caribbean Writers: A Bio-Bibliographical Critical Encyclopedia.* Three Continents Press, 1979.

This biographical-critical encyclopedia incorporates history and criticism of a number of writers from the Anglophone Caribbean.

089.   Hughes, Michael, ed. *A Companion to West Indian Literature.* London: Collins, 1979.

This text introduces the reader to the works of 106 major poets and writers from the English-speaking Caribbean. Each entry consists of a short biography and criticism, bibliography, and a select bibliography of critical writing. The text also presents a discussion of 22 important literary journals associated with the West Indies.

090.   Hughes, Roger, ed. *Caribbean Writing: A Checklist.* London: Commonwealth Institute, 1986.

This checklist is a guide to the literature holdings of the Commonwealth Institute's Library. This list which focuses on Caribbean Writing since 1960 is organized by 1) General Surveys and Criticisms, 2) Anthologies and Collections, 3) Periodicals, 4) Individual Authors, 5) Author's Country of Origin, and 6) Booksellers.

091.   Jordan, Alma and Barbara Comissiong, ed. *The English-Speaking Caribbean: A Bibliography of Bibliographies.* Boston: G. K. Hall & Co., 1984.

This bibliography lists other bibliographies up to April 1981 that deal with the lands and peoples of the former British Caribbean territories. Sixty-four categories are presented, including Literature.

092.   Lindfors, Bernth and Reinhard Sander, eds. *Dictionary of Literary Biography – Vol. 117 - Twentieth Century Caribbean and Black African Writers.* First Series. Detroit: Gale Research, 1992.

This is a compilation of literary biography on some of the best known writers of African descent.

093.   Lindfors, Bernth and Reinhard Sander, eds. *Dictionary of Literary Biography – Vol. 125 - Twentieth Century Caribbean and Black African Writers.* Second Series. Detroit: Gale Research, 1993.

This is a continuation of the compilation of literary biography on some of the best known writers of African descent.

094.   Lindfors, Bernth and Reinhard Sander, eds. *Dictionary of Literary Biography – Vol. 157 - Twentieth Century Caribbean and Black African Writers.* Third Series. Detroit: Gale Research, 1996.

This is a continuation of the compilation of literary biography on some of the best known writers of African descent.

095.   McDowell, Robert Eugene, ed. *Bibliography of Literature from Guyana.* Arlington, TX: Sable, 1975.

This bibliography contains listings of memoirs, histories, newspapers, anthropological studies, and travel books (in addition to literature listings) in explaining the complex multi-racial social and cultural climate of Guyana. The text contains the essay "The Guyana National Bookshelf (A Mini-History of Literary Guyana)" by A. J. Seymour. Each title in the bibliography has been identified by genre.

096.   Merriam, Stella E. and Joan Christiani, eds. *Commonwealth Caribbean Writers: A Bibliography.* Georgetown: Guyana Public Library, 1970.

This is a listing of works by and on (Edward) Kamau Brathwaite, Jan Carew, Wilson Harris, John Hearne, George Lamming, Vic Reid, Philip Sherlock, and Sylvia Wynter. Addresses and forewords to publications, reviews of works, biographical sketches, and information on the writers are included.

097.   New, William H., ed. *Critical Writings on Commonwealth Literatures: A Select Bibliography to 1970.* Pennsylvania State University Press, 1975.

This text contains 274 items arranged by Research Aids (General and Individual Authors). Individual authors included are Michael Anthony, Louise Bennett, L. Edward Brathwaite, Martin Carter, Austin C. Clarke, Frank A. Collymore, Wilson Harris, John Hearne, George Lamming, Edward Lucie-Smith, Claude McKay, Roger Mais, Edgar Mittelholzer, H. Orlando Patterson, Victor Reid, Jean Rhys, Andrew Salkey, Arthur J. Seymour, Louis Simpson, and Dennis Williams. Also contains a listing of theses divided by locations and individual authors.

098.   Poynting, Jeremy, ed. *East Indians in the Caribbean: A Bibliography of Imaginative Literature in English, 1894-1984.* St. Augustine, Trinidad/Tobago: Library, University of the West Indies, 1984.

This bibliography of Caribbean literature (in English) was prepared after the Third Conference on East Indians held August 29-September 5, 1984. The conference was held at the University of the West Indies, St. Augustine (Trinidad and Tobago).

099.   Walkley, Jane, ed. "A Decade of Caribbean Literary Criticism: A Select Annotated Bibliography." *Literary Half-Yearly* 11.2 (1970): 187-95.

This list contains reviews and other critical works on Caribbean authors and cultural studies. Seventeen authors are covered. All of the critical works listed appeared in the 1960's.

100.   Warwick, Ronald, ed. *Commonwealth Literature Periodicals: A Bibliography, Including Periodicals of Former Commonwealth Countries, with locations in the United Kingdom and Europe.* London: Mansell, 1979.

This compilation includes a listing of literary periodicals as well as general magazines. The text is arranged geographically. The section on the Caribbean (pp. 88-93) contains a short-title list and an alphabetical list of periodicals.

III. *Conference Proceedings*

101.   Baugh, Edward and Mervyn Morris, eds. *Progressions: West Indian Literature in the 1970s*. Kingston: Dept. of English, U.W.I., Mona, 1990.

A compilation of the proceedings (18 papers) of the Second Conference on West Indian Literature held at the University of the West Indies, Mona Campus in Jamaica in May 1982.

102.   Brown, Lloyd, ed. *The Black Writer in Africa and the Americas: Comparative Literature Conference.* 4th vol., University of Southern California, 1970.

The papers in this volume were originally delivered at the University of Southern California's Fourth Annual Conference on Comparative Literature in 1970. The conference papers by Mercer Cook, Austin Clarke, and Ismith Khan that explore cultural similarities in Blacks from North America, Africa, and the Caribbean region will be of particular interest to Caribbean scholars.

103.   Butcher, Maggie, ed. *Tibisiri: Caribbean Writers and Critics*. Denmark: Dangaroo Press, 1989.

This book emanates from the Caribbean Writers' Conference organized at the Commonwealth Institute in 1986 by Butcher. While she clearly states in the Foreword that this is not a conference report, it still captures the essence of the conference. The keynote address, papers, poems, and fiction are included. (*Tibisiri* is the name of the fibre traditionally woven by Arawak women).

104.   Cudjoe, Selwyn R., ed. *Caribbean Women Writers: Essays From The First International Conference*. Amherst: University of Massachusetts Press, 1990.

The papers in this collection were presented on April 16, 1988, at Wellesley College under the auspices of the Black Studies Department. More than fifty women writers and critics met to discuss their work. This is the first conference dedicated to the exclusive discussion of Caribbean women writers and their work.

105.   Dabydeen, David and Brinsley Samarov, eds. *India in the Caribbean*. London: Hansib, 1987.

This text collects some of the papers presented at three conferences on Indo-Caribbean history held at the University of the West Indies, 1979-1984. Also includes poems, index, and bibliography.

106.   Fiet, Lowell, ed. *West Indian Literature and Its Political Context: Proceedings*. Lowell Fiet and the College of the Humanities, University of Puerto Rico, Rio Piedras, 1988.

This publication contains proceedings of the 7th Annual Conference on West Indian Literature, March 25-28, 1987 at the University of Puerto Rico, Rio Piedras. Sessions were divided into focus areas: How Many Caribbeans?; Literature, Feminism, and Sexual Politics; Maroons; Dialect Poetry; Drama and Political Reality; and Narrative and Ideology.

107.   Gohrisch, Jana, ed. "Gender and Hybridity in Contemporary Caribbean Poetry." *Anglistentag 1997 Giessen*. Eds. Raimund Borgmeier, Herbert Grabes, and H. Andreas Jucker. Trier, Germany: Wissenschaftlicher Verlag Trier, 1998.

Proceedings at the Conference of the German Association of University Teachers of English. Issues covered include Jamaican literature from 1900-1999 and critical analyses of the works of poets Lorna Goodison, Grace Nichols, and David Dabydeen.

108.   Greene, Sue N. "Report on the Second International Conference of Caribbean Women Writers." *Callaloo* 13 (1990): 532-38.

In this short essay Greene reports on the Second International Conference of Caribbean Women Writers held in April 1990 on the St. Augustine campus of the University of the West Indies in Trinidad. She begins her exposition by comparing the second conference to the first conference held in April 1988 at Wellesley College in Massachusetts and continues with an outline of the major presenters and themes of the conference.

109. Humblestone, Eunice Bethel, ed. *Junction: An Anthology of Writing by Participants in the First Nassau Poetry Conference*. London: Macmillan Caribbean, 1987.

This is a compilation of poems and short stories presented at the First Nassau Poetry Conference in May 1985 at the College of the Bahamas.

110. Knowles, Roberta and Erika Smilowitz, eds. *Conference on Critical Approaches to West Indian Literature*. Humanities Division: College of the Virgin Islands. St. Thomas, U.S. Virgin Islands, May 1981.

A compilation of position papers (14) at the College of the Virgin Islands conference, "Critical Approaches to West Indian Literature." Presented as a joint endeavor with the University of the West Indies to facilitate scholarly research and extend professional interaction.

111. Maes-Jelinek, Hena, ed. *Commonwealth Literature and the Modern World*. Brussels: Revue Des Langues Vivantes, 1975.

The papers published in this volume were delivered at a conference on Commonwealth literature held at the University of Liege from April 2-5, 1974. The conference was organized to promote an exchange of views between members of the European branch of ACLALS and other European scholars who study and teach Commonwealth literature. Wilson Harris, Dan Jacobson, Wayne Brown, and critics from Africa, Canada, the West Indies, and the United States were in attendance.

112. McWatt, Mark A., ed. *West Indian Literature and Its Social Context*. UWI: Cave Hill, Mona, St. Augustine, College of the Virgin Islands, University of Guyana. Dept. of English, Cave Hill Campus, 1985.

Proceedings of the Fourth Annual Conference on West Indian Literature held at the Cave Hill Campus of the University of the West Indies in Barbados. Fifteen position papers by scholars/critics and post-graduate students are included. Papers are organized under the headings: "Historical Contexts," "Literature as Performance," "Naipaul and Sexality," and "Mirrors of Contemporary Society."

113.   Narasimhaiah, C. D. "A.C.L.A.L.S. Conference on Commonwealth Literature: Kingston, Jamaica, 3-9, January 1971." *Journal of Commonwealth Literature* 6.2 (Dec. 1971): 120-26.

This report captures the first A.C.L.A.L.S that was held at the University of the West Indies (Mona Campus) in Kingston as opposed to the customary British university. The conference is viewed historically as the opening chapter of a new critical agenda in West Indian Literature.

114.   Newson, Adele S. and Strong-Leek, Linda, eds. *Winds of Change: The Transforming Voices of Caribbean Women Writers and Scholars.* New York: Peter Lang, 1998.

This is a collection of selected papers presented at the 1996 International Conference of Caribbean Women Writers and Scholars at Florida International University on April 24-27.   This volume includes sixteen essays, a fictional work, and a section on Guyanese writer Beryl A. Gilroy.

115.   Pyne-Timothy, Helen, ed. *The Woman, the Writer & Caribbean Society.* Los Angeles, CA: University of California, Center for African American Studies, 1998.

The essays in this text come from a broad selection of papers presented at the Second International Conference of Caribbean Women Writers held in Trinidad in 1990. The book begins with a prologue from Jamaican writer and performer, Louise Bennett. The text is divided into six parts: History, Literature, Society, and the Struggle for Voice; Touchstones in Caribbean Women's Writing: Groundings in Myth, Ritual, and Philosophy; The Identity of the Other: Explorations of Meanings in the Works of Caribbean Women Writers; The Emergence of the Multiethnic Chorus in Caribbean Women's Writing; Exile, the Homeland, and the Caribbean Woman Writer; and The Discourse of Literary Criticism and the Work of the Caribbean Woman Writer.

116.   Salick, Roydon, ed. *The Comic Vision in West Indian Literature.* Marabella, Trinidad: [s.n.], 1993.

This is a compilation of the proceedings of the ninth Conference on West Indian Literature in St. Lucia in 1989. Deals with the comic portrayals and innuendos in the literature.

117.   Smilowitz, Erika S. and Roberta Q. Knowles, eds. *Critical Issues in West Indian Literature*. Iowa: Caribbean Books, 1984.

A compilation of papers from three regional conferences on West Indian Literature: 1st conference held in St. Thomas in 1981 focused on critical approaches to West Indian Literature; 2nd conference held in Jamaica, considered West Indian Literature since 1970; and the 3rd conference (in 1983) addressed "The Problem of Form" in West Indian Literature.

118.   Springer, Pearl Eintou, ed. *The New Aesthetic and the Meaning of Culture in the Caribbean: The Dream Coming In With The Rain*. Port of Spain, Trinidad: National Carnival Committee, CARIFESTA Secretariat, 1995.

This text collects the proceedings of the fifth CARIFESTA [Caribbean Festival of the Arts] held in Port-of-Spain, Trinidad in 1992.

119.   Thorpe, Marjorie. "Keynote Address: Second Conference of Caribbean Women Writers." *Callaloo* 13 (1990): 526-531.

This address was delivered by Dr. Marjorie Thorpe, Ambassador of Trinidad and Tobago to the United Nations, on April 24, 1990. The Second International Conference of Caribbean Women Writers took place at the St. Augustine campus at the University of the West Indies in Trinidad.

120.   *The Written Life: Biography/Autobiography in West Indian Literature: Proceedings*. Kingston: University of the West Indies, Mona Campus, 1988.

This is a collection of papers from the eighth conference on West Indian literature. Papers by Elaine Savory Fido, Ian Smith, Helen Tiffin, Evelyn O'Callaghan, Lowell Fiet, Jeffrey Robinson, Judy Rao, Colleen Cowman, Mervyn Morris, Patricia Barber, Glynne Griffith, Joyce Stewart, Samuel Soyer, Carol Boyce Davies, Carolyn Cooper, David Williams, Gordon Rohlehr, Uppinder Mehan, Lee Erwin, Roydon Salick, Roger Langen, Louis James, Selwyn Cudjoe, R. H. Lass, and Mark McWatt are included. An overview of the [entire] conference proceedings is available from the enclosed Conference Programme.

IV. Poets' (Individual) Collections

121.   Aboud, James C. *The Stone Rose.* Port of Spain, Trinidad: Paria Publishing, 1986.

A preface written by Aboud briefly details his poetic style. He contends that he is experimenting with "automatic writing" and creative absurdity as he moves apart from writing poetry that is primarily anti-colonial and anti-plantation in tone.

122.   Adisa, Opal Palmer. *Tamarind and Mango Women.* Toronto: Sister Vision, 1992.

This volume of poetry explores the Caribbean landscape through a look at its politics, social climate, and economic state in the section entitled *Tamarind.* The section entitled *Mango Women* poetically examines the Caribbean woman in a variety of situations and relationships. Poems are written in Jamaican Dialect and Standard English.

123.   Adisa, Opal Palmer and Devorah Major. *Traveling Woman.* Oakland, California: Jukebox Press, 1989.

This collection of poems is a dual effort on the part of Jamaican born poet Opal Palmer Adisa and California born writer Devorah Major. The poems speak to and celebrate the lives of women.

124.   Agard, John. *From the Devil's Pulpit*. Newcastle upon Tyne, England: Bloodaxe Books, 1997.

Agard's poetic exploration of the Devil – is presented in seven sections: Applecalypse, The Devil Leads A Busy Social Life, Where the Path Forks, Lead Us Into Temptation, The Carnal Hubbub, A Fiend of the Arts, Newspeak Devilspeak. Misunderstandings, Understandings, and New Perspectives are presented.

125.   _____. *Limbo Dancer in Dark Glasses*. Islington, England: Greenheart Press, 1983.

This collection emanates from the historical view that limbo dancing originated in the cramped quarters of the slaveships. Agard poetically reveals how this view is dramatically counter to the tourist image of limbo as a light-hearted dance.

126.   _____. *Lovelines for a Goat-born Lady*. London: Serpent's Tail, 1990.

A collection of poems with romantic love as the primary message with issues of cultural heritage, placement, and time dispersed throughout. Organized into sections entitled Blueback Memory, Creole Romance, and Through the Fingers of Time.

127.   _____. *Man to Pan*. Habana: Casa de las Americas, 1982.

This collection celebrates the growth and evolution of Steelband; it is essentially a cycle of poems to be performed with drums & steel pans. This collection was awarded the 1982 Cuban Casa de las Americas Poetry Prize.

128.   _____. *Mangoes & Bullets: Selected and New Poems 1972-1984*. London: Pluto Press, 1985.

This is a collection of new poems along with some from previous collections: *Shoot Me With Flowers* (1973), *Man to Pan* (1982), *Limbo Dancer in Dark Glasses* (1983), *Palm Tree King* (1983), and *Wanted Man* (New Poems). The author briefly discusses his work in an introduction entitled, "Himself Interviews Himself," where he (literally) interviews himself.

129.   _____. *Shoot Me With Flowers*. (self-published), 1973.

This is a self-published work. Takes a look at personal relationships and the feelings surrounding an era associated with Black Power, the Peace & Love Revolution, the Beatles, Afros, and Viet Nam.

130.   _____. *A Stone's Throw From Embankment: The South Bank Collection*. London: Royal Festival Hall, 1993.

This collection of poems was written while Agard was a Writer-in-Residence at the South Bank Centre. Poems reflect issues in the lives of Caribbeans living at home and overseas.

131.   Allen, Lillian. *Women Do This Everyday: Selected Poems*. Toronto: Women's Press, 1993.

This collection of Allen's poems celebrates the various expressions and emotions of women. The volume is divided into sections: She would sing liberation, Sheroes, dreams & history, Somewhere in this slivered city, Dis, Conditions Critical, The life of a sound, and A mek wi. An introduction by Allen outlines the development of dub poetry.

132.   _____. *Rhythm an' Hardtimes*. Toronto: Domestic Bliss, 1982.

This is a small collection of thirteen poems which the author contends are meant for performance as well as the printed page. Lillian Allen, from Jamaica, is popularly known as having introduced Dub poetry to Canada.

133.   Armstrong, Ivy Claudette. *Native Dawta*. Kingston: Kingston Publishers, 1995.

This collection of poems is primarily written in dialect reminiscent of the style of the renowned poet Louise Bennett. Poems evoke memories of life in Jamaica. Divided into five sections: Dung A Yawd, Gal An' Bwoy, Nyammins, Farrin Worries, and Holiness Unto De Lawd.

134.   Arthur, Kevin Alan. *England and Nowhere*. Leeds: Peepal Tree, 1993.

Arthur takes his title *England and Nowhere* from T. S. Eliot's *Little Gidding*. A collection of thirty + poems; includes a prelude and explanatory notes on Caribbean terms, culture, etc.

135.   Baugh, Edward. *A Tale From The Rainforest*. Jamaica: Sandberry Press, 1988.

This collection of 41 poems is written by Baugh, a critic, poet, and educator at the University of the West Indies (Mona Campus). Poems of introspection and foresight make up the collection.

136.   _____. *It Was The Singing.* Toronto and Kingston: Sandberry Press, 2000.

This volume includes all of the poems from Baugh's first collection, A *Tale From The Rainforest* along with 31 new poems. Poems range from the lighthearted to intensely emotional.

137.   Bennett, Louise. *Anancy and Miss Lou.* Kingston, 1979.

This text, written in Jamaican Creole, contains variations of the Anancy tales as told by Miss Lou. The tales are accompanied by songs and sheet music.

138.   _____. *Auntie Roachie seh.* Ed. Mervyn Morris. Kingston, Jamaica: Sangster's Book Stores, 1993.

This volume contains fifty humorous radio dialogues from a series presented by Louise Bennett between 1965 and 1982. Written in Jamaican Creole, the dialogues deal with topical subjects and also include a number of Jamaican proverbs. A short but illuminating introduction by Morris provides insight on the language and content. A glossary is also provided.

139.   _____. *Selected Poems: Louise Bennett.* Ed. Mervyn Morris. Kingston, Jamaica: Sangster's Book Stores , 1982.

This collection of poems by Bennett has been edited, with an introduction, notes, and teaching questions (by Mervyn Morris). An effort has been made to broaden the audience for Bennett's work through the carefully crafted prefatory material and glossary at the end of the text.

140.   Berry, James. *Fractured Circles.* London: New Beacon, 1979.

This collection of selected poems reflects Berry's life and subsequent evolution over twenty years in England. The poems reflect a strong mingling of Caribbean Creole and Standard English.

141.   _____. *Hot Earth Cold Earth.* Newcastle upon Tyne: Bloodaxe Books, 1995.

This book contains new poems as well as poems from the collection, *Chain of Days* (now out of print). The poems speak to the poet's divided life as an "outsider," a man speaking two languages – 'Hot Earth' Creole and 'Cold Earth' English.

142.   _____. *Lucy's Letters and Loving.* London: New Beacon, 1982.

This collection of poems grew out of a "light-hearted" conversation Berry had with a West Indian female colleague who was [then] currently living in London. The poems are cast in the form of letters "Lucy" sends back home [a small Caribbean village] to her friend about the life she currently lives and the one she misses back home. Divided into two sections: Loving and Lucy's Letters.

143.   _____. *Chain of Days.* Oxford: Oxford University Press, 1985.

This collection of 63 poems is divided into six topical sections: Chain of Days, Fantasy of an African Boy, Parts and Wholeness, Reconsidering, Thinking Back on Yard Time, and Approach and Response. The poems deal with the relationships between the colonized and the colonizer and the type of person created by such a relationship.

144.   _____. *When I Dance.* London: Hamish Hamilton, 1988.

The poems in this collection were written over a period of five years when Berry was attempting to create [writing] models in workshops with young people. The poems reflect the rural life of the Caribbean as well as the inner-city life of Britain. The text is illustrated by Sonia Boyce.

145.   Black, Ayanna. *No Contingencies.* Toronto: Williams-Wallace, 1986.

Black explores the lives of Caribbean women of African descent in Canada. Divided into three sections: A Sense of Origin, Touch, and Freedom Dance. The poet blends patois and standard English in this poetic exploration of life in the Caribbean Diaspora.

146.   Bloom, Valerie. *Duppy Jamboree and Other Jamaican Poems.* Cambridge University Press, 1992.

A collection of performance poetry written in modified Jamaican patois. This collection reflects on the highs and lows of childhood and growth in the Caribbean.

147.   _____. *Touch Mi, Tell Mi*. London: Bogle-L'Ouverture Publications, 1983.

A brief introduction by Linton Kwesi Johnson explains Bloom's poetic style – the use of nation speech with an emphasis on rural versus urban expressions. This is Bloom's first volume of poems. The poems are largely about Jamaican rural and village life and are written in the humorous style of Louise Bennett.

148.   Brand, Dionne. *Chronicles of the Hostile Sun*. Toronto: Williams-Wallace, 1984.

Brand chronicles military conflict in the Caribbean region by creating poetry that focuses on the angst of people striving for selfhood, nationhood – identity. Organized into sections entitled Languages, Sieges, and Military Occupations.

149.   _____. *Earth Magic: Poetry for Young People*. Toronto: Sister Vision Press, 1991.

This collection of 24 poems is written for young children. Each poem is illustrated by the artist Veronica Sullivan.

150.   _____. *Fore Day Morning*. Toronto: Khoisan Artists, 1978.

This is Brand's first published work in book form. Born in Trinidad, she is well-known as a performance poet throughout Canada. This collection of 25 poems reflect her cultural heritage and her new North American home.

151.   _____. *Land to Light On*. Toronto: McClelland & Stewart, 1997.

This is Brand's first book of poems since her collection *No Language is Neutral*, short-listed for The Governor General's Award in 1990. This collection focuses on her life [and that of other Caribbeans] living in Canada.

152.   _____. *No Language Is Neutral*. Toronto: Coach House Press, 1990.

Brand explores the possibilities of power and communication through the poetry in this collection which was short listed for The Governor General's Award in 1990.

153.   _____. *Primitive Offensive*. Toronto: Williams-Wallace, 1982.

Organized into fourteen cantos, Brand's poems are riveting examples of womanist protest against colonialistic oppression. The poems expose the concerns of women in the Caribbean, Canada, and throughout the world.

154.   _____. *Winter Epigrams and Epigrams to Ernesto Cardinal in Defence of Claudia*. Toronto: Williams-Wallace, 1983.

These epigrams are written [by Brand] in a latter response to the epigrams written by Ernesto Cardinal [Nicaraguan priest, poet, Marxist, and humanist] to Claudia, a woman he was, supposedly, in love with. Brand deftly moves between the real and the symbolic in her use of Claudia as subject.

155.   Brathwaite, Edward Kamau. *The Arrivants: A New World Trilogy*. London: Oxford University Press, 1973.

This trilogy is organized into three distinct yet related books: *Rights of Passage, Islands,* and *Masks*. Each division is a poetic examination of phases of intrinsic understanding through movement, both physical and spiritual. Brathwaite's physical journey to Africa serves as the foundation of this major contribution to the prominence of the Anglophone Caribbean poetry canon.

156.   _____. *Black & Blues*. La Habana, Cuba: Casa de las Americas, 1976.

A collection of poems which explores the issue of fragmentation in island societies where slavery and colonialism have left indelible imprints. Brathwaite juxtaposes the fragmentation of the Caribbean region against the power of "a fusion of laughter, tragedy, bitter complaint, religious ecstasy, desperation, and an unconquerable world to survive"- in short, a rendition of the "blues" and its cathartic force. Organized into three parts: "Fragments," "Drought," and "Flowers."

157.   _____. *Dream Stories* (with an introduction by Gordon Rohlehr). Essex, England: Longman, 1974.

Dream Stories grew out of three centrally dramatic events in Brathwaite's life: the death of his wife Doris; the devastation of his home, personal archives, and library during Hurricane Gilbert; and his personal encounter with robbers in his flat in Kingston. These life-altering events led to this collection which is a composite of poetry, narrative, and "dream-talk" with the motif of journey at its core. Organized into seven sections: "The Black Angel," "Dream Chad," "Dream Crabs," "4ᵗʰ Traveller," "Dream Haiti," "Grease," and "Salvages."

158.   _____. *Islands*. London: Oxford University Press, 1970.

This is the third book of Brathwaite's trilogy, *The Arrivants*. A poetic discussion, the issue of African Caribbean "rootlessness" permeates the five sections: New World, Limbo, Rebellion, Possession, and Beginning. Empowerment informs the synthesis of the sections which discuss African Caribbeans' social, political, economic, and religious psyche.

159.   _____. *Masks*. London: Oxford University Press, 1968.

This is the second book of Brathwaite's trilogy *The Arrivants*. This section focuses on knowledge and understanding acquired through a journey [physical and metaphysical] back to Africa.

160.   _____. *Middle Passages*. Newcastle upon Tyne: Bloodaxe Books, 1992.

This collection of poetry embodies a political tone with notes of poetic revolution and protest. Brathwaite extends his political commentary with poems on Nicolas Guillen, Mikey Smith, the Maroons, Kwame Nkrumah, Walter Rodney, and Nelson Mandela. The unmistakable influence of music in Caribbean life is examined with references to Black musicians Duke Ellington and Bessie Smith.

161.   _____. *Mother Poem*. London: Oxford University Press, 1977.

In the preface to this collection of 25 poems, Brathwaite states that the work "is about porous limestone: my mother, Barbados: most English of West Indian Islands, but at the same time nearest, as the slaves fly, to Africa." The collection is divided into four sections: "Rock Seed," "Nightwash," "Tuk," and Koumfort."

162.   _____. *Other Exiles*. London: Oxford University Press, 1975.

This collection of short[er] poems was written over a 25 year period. Like his trilogy, *The Arrivants*, the poems in this collection use journey as the central motif. The journey is described poetically through the poet's movement from home [Barbados] to Europe and home again.

163. _____. *Rights of Passage*. London: Oxford University Press, 1967.

This is the "inaugural" book of Brathwaite's trilogy *The Arrivants*. This section of the trilogy sets the stage for the movement from "home" [the Caribbean] to "home" [Africa] and "home" [the Caribbean] again.

164. _____. *Sappho Sakyi's Meditations*. Mona: Savacou Publications, 1989.

This was the beginning of a series of *Savacou Versions* where poets were invited to send in "lost poems, well-known poems, or those they felt were important." The Sappho Sayki sequence was first published in *Bim* 26 (1958).

165. _____. *Shar, Hurricane Poem*. Mona: Savacou, 1990.

This poem was written when Brathwaite heard news of an approaching hurricane in Jamaica. He equates the devastation of the hurricane with that of an unrecorded cultural history. This poem can be heard on a Watershed Tapes recording, *Atumpan* (1989).

166. _____. *Sun Poem*. London: Oxford University Press, 1982.

A complement to his trilogy (consisting also of *Mother Poem* and *X/Self*), *Sun (Son) Poem* places emphasis on maleness and its various constructs. Browns Beach is the main setting of the poem (the sunset side of the island) which is in dramatic contrast to the Atlantic sea coast in *Mother Poem*.

167. _____. *Third World Poems*. London: Longman Group Ltd., 1983.

Organized into three sections entitled L'Ouverture, Ashanty Town, and Irie, some of these poems have appeared previously in other collections by Brathwaite. A refreshing presentation of highlights from major works such as *Sun Poem, Black + Blues, Rights of Passage,* and *Islands*.

168. _____. *Trench Town Rock*. Providence: Lost Roads Publishers, 1994.

This volume presents a sharp poetic look at life and violence in Jamaica. Divided into six sections: The Marley Manor Shoot/in, Straight Talk, Kingston in the Kingdom of This World, My Turn, Short History of Dis, and Anansese. Brathwaite's "Sycorax video-print" style of typesetting is featured.

169.   _____. *X/Self.* London: Oxford University Press, 1987.

Divided into five sections, this collection is a part of his trilogy which contains *Mother Poem* and *Sun Poem.* The text contains notes to promote insight on Caribbean cultural terms. Poems of deep introspection comprise this collection.

170.   _____. *The Zea Mexican Diary.* The University of Wisconsin Press, 1993.

A combination of diary entries and letters, this collection chronicles the impact of the death of Brathwaite's wife, Doris Monica, on his life and his work. Sandra Poucher Paquet writes the foreword to this collection.

171.   Breeze, Jean "Binta." *Answers.* Masani Productions, 1983.

This volume represents Breeze's early work as a poet. These 15 poems cover a wide range of societal concerns with a hint of militancy. Breeze is now well-known as a performance poet and dub artist.

172.   _____. *The Arrival of Brighteye and Other Poems.* Newcastle upon Tyne: Bloodaxe Books, 2000.

This collection of 31 poems can be classified as Caribbean songs. The works reflect Breeze's memories as a child growing up in the hilly region of Jamaica.

173.   _____. *On The Edge Of An Island.* Newcastle upon Tyne: Bloodaxe Books, 1997.

This collection of twenty-eight works is a collage of poetry and short stories. Some included works were previously published by Serpent's Tail and 57 Productions.

174.   _____. *Riddym Ravings and Other Poems.* Ed. Mervyn Morris. London: Race Today Publications, 1988.

This collection of 38 poems showcases Breeze's ability to move smoothly among standard English, Jamaican patois, and Dub technique in the creation of her poetry.

175.   _____. *Spring Cleaning.* London: Virago Press, 1992.

This collection of fifty poems reflects Breeze's background as a dub poet yet moves beyond as she draws upon her rural roots in Sandy Bay, Jamaica. The popular poem 'Riddym Ravings...' is included in this collection.

176.   Brown, Beverly E. *Dream Diary*. Kingston, Jamaica: Savacou, 1982.

This slim volume of nineteen poems reflects a vivid use of intertwined imagery and philosophy. The collection contains a short preface written by the poet.

177.   Brown, Lloyd Wellesley. *Duppies*. Leeds: Peepal Tree Press, 1996.

This is a collection of 28 poems which maintains the "duppy imagery" from beginning to end. "Libations," the opening poem, showcases Brown's poetic techniques.

178.   Brown, Raymond Waldin. *Bahamas in Poetry and Prose*. Bahamas, 1970.

In the Foreword to this collection, H.W. Brown contends that the poems contained within were written "to fill a gap not hitherto undertaken since the days of the late Williams Christie, Poet Laureate of the Bahamas." Paintings by Merna Sheldon of Bahamian scenes are included.

179.   Brown, Wayne. *On the Coast*. London: Andre Deutsch, 1972.

This slim volume consists of 20 + poems dedicated to Derek Walcott. A number of the poems have appeared in journals such as *Bim, Jamaica Journal,* and *Breaklight,* among others.

180.   _____. *Voyages*. Port of Spain, Trinidad: Inprint Caribbean Ltd., 1989.

These poems are reflections of a life as seen through a series of journeys or voyages to understanding and truth. The collection of 55 poems is divided into two sections.

181.   Campbell, George. *First Poems*. New York: Garland Publishing, 1981.

This collection of "first" poems contain messages of defiance and coming to terms with change. It was first published in 1945 in Kingston, Jamaica.

182.   _____. *Earth Testament*. Kingston, Jamaica: George Campbell Associates, 1983.

This volume of 80 + poems contains an introduction by Edward Baugh, poet and critic. Baugh briefly discusses the evolution of Campbell's poetry from themes of defiance to a more cosmic and elemental poetic delivery.

183.　　Carberry, H. D. *It Takes A Mighty Fire.* Kingston: Ian Randle Publishers, 1995.

Along with his well known poem, "It Takes A Mighty Fire," 45 other poems are included in this collection. A foreword by Sir Philip Sherlock and an introduction by Edward Baugh complement the compilation.

184.　　Carew, Jan. *Sea Drums in My Blood.* Port of Spain, Trinidad and Tobago: The New Voices, 1980.

This is Carew's first published collection of poems and includes the first poem Carew wrote. Poems focus on themes of exile, struggle, love, death, and Africa.

185.　　Carter, Martin. *Poems of Affinity.* Georgetown, Guyana: Release, 1980.

These poems reflect the private and public sides of Carter. A foreword by Bill Carr provides insights on Carter's writing techniques and his status as Guyana's finest poet. A collection of 35 poems of which only one is overtly political.

186.　　_____. *Poems of Resistance from Guyana.* Georgetown, Guyana: Release, 1979.

First published in 1954 under the title *Poems of Resistance from British Guiana.* These poems address British colonial control of Guyana in the 1950s and the resistance of those people oppressed by such control.

187.　　_____. *Poems of Succession.* London: New Beacon Books, 1977.

This collection combines works from previous collections: *The Hill of Fire Glows Red, The Kind Eagle, Returning, Poems of Resistance, Poems of Shape and Motion, Conversations,* and *Jail Me Quickly.*

188.　　_____. *Selected Poems.* Georgetown, Guyana: Demerara Publishers Ltd., 1989.

According to Ian McDonald who writes the foreword to this collection, "This book contains those of his published poems which Martin Carter now wishes to collect and make more easily available. The major collections of his poems – *Poems of Resistance, Poems of Succession, Poems of Affinity* – are out of print." McDonald's foreword provides biographical and critical information about Carter and his writing.

189.   Chan, Brian. *Thief with Leaf.* Leeds: Peepal Tree Press, 1988.

This collection of 45 poems has a meditative quality in its exposure of everyday occurrences and emotions. Chan, a Guyanese, is also a painter and musician. His musical and visual arts background are reflected in his poetic style.

190.   _____. *Fabula Rasa.* Leeds: Peepal Tree Press, 1994.

This collection illustrates an expansion in Chan's poetic style from his earlier collection, *Thief with Leaf.* The poems are grouped into four sections: Fiction, Deserts, The Book, and The Verbless Time.

191.   Changa, Ras. *Illegal Truth.* St. Martin: House of Nehesi, 1991.

An introduction by Rita Celestine captures and celebrates the essence of Changa's first published collection which is divided into four chapters: Beach Head, Changes, Sounds, and Mystic Noon. Changa is referred to by Celestine as a "quietly, forceful Rastafarian."

192.   Charles, Faustin. *Crab Track.* London: Brookside Press, 1973.

The crab in its multiple motions and activities is used as the initial motif (followed by other life forms) to explore a full range of life issues. A collection of 34 poems some of which have appeared in *Breaklight, Bim, Time Out, Caribbean Quarterly, Savacou, Focus,* etc.

193.   _____. *Days and Nights in the Magic Forest.* London: Bogle L'Ouverture, 1986.

This volume of poems has a magical quality as Charles weaves myth, folklore, and reality in depicting a physical, mental, and emotional terrain that is uniquely Caribbean. A collection of 35 poems.

194.   Clark, LeRoy. *Taste of Endless Fruit, Love Poems, and Drawings.* Port of Spain, Trinidad: Aquarela Galleries for KaRaEle, 1992.

A collection of love poems and drawings. Poems are written in calligraphy. Clark employs the literary and the visual in this presentation.

195.   Cliff, Michelle. *Claiming An Identity They Taught Me To Despise.* Waketown, Mass: Persephone Press, 1980.

This volume of prose poetry explores the female search for identity and wholeness. Divided into sections: Passing, Filaments, Obsolete Geography, Accurate Record, Against Granite, A History of Costume, Women's Work, Claiming An Identity They Taught Me to Despise, The Garden, and Separations.

196.   _____. *The Land of Look Behind*. New York: Firebrand, 1985.

This is a collection of prose and poetry. Dedicated to Audre Lorde, the collection contains a preface entitled "A Journey Into Speech" wherein Cliff explains her "coming to" poetic writing.

197.   Collins, Merle. *Because the Dawn Breaks*. London: Karia Press, 1985.

This collection of poems carries the subtitle, "Poems Dedicated to the Grenadian People." Ngugi Wa Thiong'o writes the introduction to this collection of 30+ poems which is accompanied by photographs.

198.   _____. *Rotten Pomerack*. London: Virago, 1992.

Collins' poetry underscores her continued love for her homeland and its people. The poems in this volume are mini-stories, both personal and political, that have their origin in the Caribbean and continue in England.

199.   Collymore, Frank A. *Selected Poems*. Barbados: Coles Printery Ltd., 1971.

Collymore collects poems written in the 1940's (with the exception of two) in this text. The collection illustrates the range of his writing over the years.

200.   Cooper, Afua. *Breaking Chains*. Toronto: Weelahs Publications, 1984.

These poems reflect Cooper's experience as a Black Rasta woman. In her Preface, the poet explains that "breaking chains" holds three symbolic meanings, which are bound up in her femaleness and Blackness.

201.   _____. *Memories Have Tongue*. Toronto: Sister Vision Press, 1992.

This collection of poems was written over a six-year period, 1985-1991. Cooper contends in the Preface that these poems explore the personal and the public, the past and the present. She looks at her experiences as a black woman from the Caribbean now living in Canada.

202. _____. *The Red Caterpillar on College Street.* Toronto: Sister Vision Press, 1989.

This volume of poems was written by Cooper for all the children who live in the inner city of Toronto. The text is illustrated by Stephanie Martin.

203. Craig, Christine. *Quadrille for Tigers.* California: Mina Press, 1984.

This book contains 50+ poems, some of which have appeared previously in *Good News, Savacou, Arts Review,* and *Hambone* magazines and the anthology *Jamaica Woman.*

204. Craig, Dennis. *Near the Seashore.* Guyana: Education and Development Services, Inc., 1999.

This collection of poetry is the winner of the 1998 Guyana Prize for Literature for the Best First Book of Poetry. Some of Craig's poems have appeared in a number of anthologies, yet this is the first collection of his work.

205. Dabydeen, Cyril. *Born in Amazonia.* Ontario: Mosaic Press, 1995.

Dabydeen's collection addresses as well as synthesizes South American and Canadian life and beliefs as he examines the power of the jaguar and its mythic proportions in South America. The collection is organized into sections entitled The Leap that takes the ground by surprise, Gathering Dust to Stop the Ocean, Crocodiles and Canons, and Kidneys Twinned and Remembering.

206. _____. *Coastland: New and Selected Poems (1973-1987).* Oakville: Mosaic Press, 1989.

This collection gathers some of Cyril Dabydeen's new poetry along with selected material published between 1973 and 1987. A brief introduction by Jeremy Poynting provides a view on Dabydeen's artistic development.

207. _____. *Discussing Columbus.* London: Peepal Tree Press, 1997.

Dabydeen poetically explores Columbus's 1492 "mistake" in thinking he had landed in India when in actuality he had landed in the Caribbean. Dabydeen divides this collection into four sections: Adrift, The Hidden Sun, Rites, and The Caribbees.

208.   _____. *Distances*. Vancouver, B.C.: Fiddlehead Poetry Books, 1977.

This is an early collection of Cyril Dabydeen's poetry. Seventeen poems cover topics that range from the search for identity, nostalgia for home, and elements of loss. Notable early poems are "Poet Speaks to the House" and "After the Rain."

209.   _____. *Elephants Make Good Stepladders*.   London: Third Eye Publications, 1982.

This is Dabydeen's sixth collection of poetry. The elephant is the central, recurring motif in this collection that blends the world of the Caribbean with that of his new home, Canada.

210.   _____. *Heart's Frame: Poems*. Cornwall, Ontario: Vesta Publications Limited, 1979.

This is a large collection of more than 60 poems organized into three sections: Open Spaces, Shapes and Shadows, and Tropics.

211.   _____. *Islands Lovelier Than A Vision*. London: Peepal Tree Press, 1986.

This collection of 45 poems is divided into four sections: ...the meandering self, ...a realist's touch, ...in a limbo world, and ...marred with upheaval. The poetry is reflective of Dabydeen's present life in Canada informed by his Guyanese past.

212.   _____. *Poems in Recession*. Georgetown, Guyana: Sadeek Press, 1972.

A. J. Seymour writes the Foreword in this slender volume of early poetry by Cyril Dabydeen. Seymour comments on Dabydeen's themes and his promise as a major writer. "Poem to Your Own," winner of the A. J. Seymour Prize 1967, is included.

213.   _____. *Stoning the Wind*. Toronto: TSAR, 1994.

This collection of poems by Dabydeen is divided into four parts: At the Bend, Who We Are, An Old Sky, and Talking Again. Dabydeen's Asian, Caribbean, and Canadian backgrounds are present in his work which ranges from the simplistic to the dramatic.

214.   Dabydeen, David. *Coolie Odyssey*. London: Hansib Publishing and Dangaroo Press, 1990.

This collection of poems by Dabydeen was published to mark the 150th anniversary of Indians in the Caribbean. These poems represent the journey of East Indians from India to Guyana to England. This work was begun by the poet on a train journey from Edinburgh to Birmingham.

215.   _____. *Slave Song*. Sydney: Dangaroo Press, 1984.

This poetry presents the range of emotions and experiences of East Indians in the Caribbean laboring under indenture. Contains notes on Creoles and Pidgins; English based. Background on Guyanese plantation life is provided in the introduction.

216.   _____. *Turner: New and Selected Poems*. London: Jonathan Cape, 1994.

A collection of poetry based on a painting, "Slavers Throwing Overboard the Dead and Dying," of M. W. Turner exhibited in 1840 at the Royal Academy. In the preface Dabydeen contends, "The intensity of Turner's painting is such that I believe the artist in private must have savoured the sadism he publicly denounced."

217.   D'Aguiar, Fred. *Airy Hall*. London: Chatto & Windus, 1989.

D'Aguiar follows the pattern in his earlier collection, *Mama Dot* in dividing his poems into three sections. Part One explores "Airy Hall," Part Two includes riveting poems such as "Only the President's Eggs Are Yellow," and Part Three is devoted to a rather long poetic discourse, "The Kitchen Bitch" (a three-tiered lamp formerly used by Jamaican peasants who could not afford other forms of lighting). This book was awarded the Guyana Prize for Poetry.

218.   _____. *British Subjects*. Bloodaxe Books, 1993.

This is D'Aguiar's third book of poems; he follows the same triad structure of organization utilized in previous works. Poems such as "At the Grave of the Unknown African," SOS," and "Bone Flute" are showcases of his poetic talent.

219.   _____. *Mama Dot*. London: Chatto & Windus, 1985.

This collection is organized into three parts: Mama Dot, Roots Broadcast, and Guyanese Days. The collection starts with a poem of survival, "Mama Dot," the title of this collection. Includes a brief glossary of dialect words to increase accessibility of meaning. This book won a Poetry Book Society Recommendation.

220.   Das, Mahadai. *Bones*. Yorkshire: Peepal Tree Press, 1989.

This collection of twenty-eight poems provides a look at the impact of movement on the spirit and everyday life of Caribbean people.

221.   _____. *My Finer Steel Will Grow*. Richford, Vt.: Samisdat, 1982.

These poems reflect Das's militant stance on the past, present, and future of life in Guyana. Poems also contain projections/possibilities of life outside of Guyana yet with an on-going sensibility and understanding of the past.

222.   _____. *I Want To Be A Poetess of My People*. Guyana: National History and Arts Council, n.d.

The ten poems in this small volume are militant in tone. Themes of revolution and change in Guyana permeate Das's poetic delivery.

223.   Dawes, Kwame. *Jacko Jacobus*. Leeds: Peepal Tree Press, 1996.

Some of the poems in this collection have appeared (in various forms) in the *Mississippi Review*, The *London Review of Books*, and *Obsidian II*. An epic journey of love, deceit, murder, and faith through the experiences and insights of Jacko Jacobus, "father of nations." Dawes uses the myth of Jacob and Esau as his foundation to explore unrealized strivings.

224.   _____. *Progeny of Air*. Leeds: Peepal Tree Books, 1994.

The salmon in its various positions is used as the central motif in this poetic collection which reflects on Dawes' Ghanian birth, life in Jamaica, Canadian education, and present life in South Carolina. Poems are narrative infused with a dramatic sense of spatial and chronological focus. This collection won the Forward Poetry Prize for the best collection of 1994.

225.   _____. *Prophets*. Leeds: Peepal Tree Press, 1995.

This is Dawes third collection of poetry. In each of the three sections of this collection of 27 poems, he focuses on the centrality of prophecy in the life cycle. *Prophets* is a revealing epic poem of the various prophetic powers of the characters, Clarice and Thalbot. "The Making of a Prophet," and "Flight" are illustrative of Dawes' poetic style.

226.   _____. *Requiem.* Leeds: Peepal Tree Press, 1996.

These poems were inspired by the illustrations of Tom Feeling in *The Middle Passage: White Ships/Black Cargo.* A collection of 26 poems which explore the range of feelings attendant with a remembrance of the plight of the millions of victims of transatlantic slavery.

227.   _____. *Shook Foil.* Leeds: Peepal Tree Press, 1997.

Poetic musings about Bob Marley, family, and self-knowledge with the beat of reggae commanding the pages.   Spliced with fifteen poems entitled "Tentative Definitions I–XV."

228.   Douglas, Marcia. *Electricity Comes to Cocoa Bottom.* Leeds: Peepal Tree Press, 1999.

This volume of poetry begins with the image of the voicelessness of the country people of Cocoa Bottom who experience the coming of electricity to their part of the world. Douglas places emphasis on the journey toward a voice.

229.   Dunn-Smith, Dana B. E. *Faces in the Sun: A Selection of Magnificent Poetry.* Kingston: Bodile & Siapoe, 1990.

This volume of poetry places emphasis on the spiritual self. Poems are organized in four sections: Political, Social, Mystical, and Romance. Jamaican-born Dunn-Smith currently resides and works in Bermuda.

230.   Escoffery, Gloria. *Landscape in the Making.* Jamaica: 1976.

This, Escoffery's first volume of poetry, consists of six poems. The poems reflect an individual coming of age, which evokes a vivid picture of the Caribbean landscape and the poetic persona's relationship with that landscape.

231.   _____. *Loggerhead.* Kingston, Jamaica: Sandberry Press, 1988.

Perhaps better known as a painter than a poet, Escoffery's works in *Loggerhead* show her command of visual imagery as translated onto the printed page. Some of the poems in this collection have appeared in *The Daily Gleaner, Caribbean Voices, Breaklight, Caribbean Poetry Now, The Penguin Book of Caribbean Verse,* and *Bim.*

232.   _____. *Mother Jackson Murders the Moon*. Leeds: Peepal Tree Press, 1998.

The poetry in this volume covers a variety of moods and emotions from happiness to uncertainty. Poetic characters and the poetic persona are vividly presented by Escoffery.

233.   Espinet, Ramabai. *Nuclear Seasons*. Toronto: Sister Vision Press, 1991.

This volume of poetry reveals Espinet's Indo-Caribbean background, as well as her current life in Canada. The collection is divided into three sections: Hosay Night, A Nowhere Place, and Equitable Landings. A glossary of terms, helpful to readers new to Caribbean poetry, completes the volume.

234.   Fergus, Howard A. *Calabash of Gold*. London: Linda Lee Books, 1993.

E. A. Markham writes the introduction to this volume of poetry, which represents Fergus's work published in separate volumes over a number of years. Markham comments on Fergus's poetic styling through a mini-analysis of the section of the book, *Visitation*. Divided into seven sections: Colonial Calabash, Village Life, Belongers, Visitation, Occasional Poems, In Memoriam, and Politics for Sport.

235.   _____. *Cotton Rhymes*. Plymouth, Montserrat: Alliouagana Commune, 1976.

This early collection of Fergus's poetry contains 28 poems which deal with a variety of issues: love, politics, migration, and celebrations.

236.   _____. *Green Innocence*. Plymouth, Montserrat: University of the West Indies Extra-Mural Dept., 1978.

This is Fergus's second collection of poems. An introduction written by Jane Grell (Librarian, Montserrat Public Library) classifies these poems as deeply conscious and intense. A collection of 38 poems.

237.   _____. *Lara Rains of Colonial Rites*. Leeds: Peepal Tree Press, 1998.

This volume of poetry explores the irony of Montserrat's movement away from its colonial ties through the celebration of a very white, very colonial game, cricket. Brian Lara's importance to Montserrat is celebrated as Fergus continues the search for power over a past informed by the dominance of slavery and colonialism.

238.   Figueroa, John. *The Chase: A Collection of Poems, 1941-1989*. Leeds: Peepal Tree, 1991.

This collection presents a look at poems that span Figueroa's writing career. New works occur alongside many poems that have been published before in anthologies, journals, and in Figueroa's earlier collections, *Love Leaps Here* and *Ignoring Hurts*.

239.   _____. *Ignoring Hurts: Poems*. Washington, D.C.: Three Continents Press, 1976.

An introduction by Frank Getlein explains Figuero's writing style and his range of thematic concerns. The erotic impulse of life is captured in his title poem "Ignoring Hurts," among others.

240.   Franklyn, Omowale David. *Tongue of Another Drum*. Grenada: Talented House Publications, 1994.

In the introduction, Victor L. Chang introduces Franklyn as "a young Grenadian finding his poetic voice." The motif of the drum (as a recognition of his connection to an African heritage) appears as a small icon on alternate pages of this collection organized into Part One, Interlude, and Part Two.

241.   Fraser, Reginald, Jr. *Cycle: A Selection of Poems*. Kingston, Jamaica: Deryck Roberts Consultant Ltd., 1991.

Fraser says, in his introduction, that these poems represent an "intensely personal chronicle." The poet arranges the poems in the order in which they were written in a journey of a quarter century.

242.   Gabbadios, W. *Jamaica Dawn: Powerful Perceptions of Our Land*. Kingston: Jamrite Publications, 1991.

This volume of poetry and short prose renders a celebratory story of the people and the landscape of Jamaica. The works evoke the symbolism of the Jamaican flag of black, green, and gold.

243.   Gonzales, Anson. *Collected Poems*. Trinidad and Tobago: The New Voices, 1979.

In his Preface, Gonzalez contends that the poems in this volume represent his work at the end of Phase One of his development as a writer. The introduction by Dr. Geraldine Bobb (of the Ministry of Education and Culture, Trinidad and Tobago) explains the seven parts of the collection: The Art, Briefs, Kindergarten, Boysie, Blues, Nationstate, and Daimonic.

244.   _____. *Merry-Go-Round and other Poems.* Trinidad and Tobago: The New Voices, 1992.

This collection of Gonzalez's poems is one of the Carifesta presentations of The New Voices. Most of the poems in this collection have appeared in other collections by Gonzalez – *Collected Poems* (1979) and *Moksha: Poems of Light and Sound* (1988).

245.   _____. *Moksha: Poems of Light and Sound.* Trinidad and Tobago: The New Voices, 1988.

Most of the poems in this collection can be found in Gonzalez's 1984 volume, *Postcards & Haiku.* A few new poems are featured in this work, which is divided into four sections: Epistles, Postcards, Haiku, and Contemplations.

246.   Goodison, Lorna. *Heartease.* London: New Beacon, 1988.

A collection of 33 poems. The collection contains four variations of a poem entitled "Heartease...," two variations of a poem entitled "Star Suite...," and two variations of "A Rosary of Your Names..."

247.   _____. *I Am Becoming My Mother.* London: New Beacon, 1986.

A collection of poems which survey and celebrate womanhood and strength. Includes poems for Jean Rhys and Rosa Parks.

248.   _____. *Lorna Goodison: The Commonwealth of Letters Readings, Number 1.* New York: CUNY, 1995.

This collection of poems was published on the occasion of a reading by the poet on December 12, 1989 at the Research Institute for the Study of Man, New York, New York.

249.   _____. *Selected Poems.* University of Michigan Press, 1992.

This is a compilation of Goodison's work over the years which have appeared in some of her other collections as well as various anthologies.

250.   _____. *Tamarind Season.* Kingston, Jamaica: Institute of Jamaica Publications, 1980.

This volume of poems reflects Goodison's womanist viewpoints on various aspects of life including love, family, politics, and the economy. This collection of over 50 poems is illustrated by the poet.

251.   _____. *To Us, All Flowers Are Roses: Poems*. Urbana: Univ. of Illinois Press, 1995.

This gathering of poems by Goodison focuses on her homeland and various issues (social, political, economic, etc.) surrounding memories of people and events. Some of these poems have appeared in *The Hudson Review, Saturday Night, Nimrod, The Literary Review, Caribbean Quarterly, Kyk-Over-Al, Wasafiri, Jamaica Journal, and Litera Pur.*

252.   _____. *Turn Thanks*. Urbanna, Chicago: University of Illinois Press, 1999.

This collection of poems is divided into four sections: My Mother's Sea Chanty, This Is My Father's Country, The Mango of Poetry, and God a Me.

253.   Goulbourne, Jean L. *Actors in the Arena*. Kingston, Jamaica: Savacou Cooperative, 1977.

This volume of 20 poems combines Goulbourne's early poetry with her more recent work. Poems such as "One Acre" reflect her association with the land, while the poem "Politics" reflects social and political inequities. A foreword is written by Edward Kamau Brathwaite.

254.   _____. *Under the Sun*. Trinidad & Tobago: New Voices, 1992.

A short collection of twenty poems that was first published in 1988. Poems focus on the varied worldview of Jamaican life.

255.   Gray, Cecil *Leaving The Dark*. Toronto, Ontario: Lilibel Publications, 1998.

This third book of poems by Gray reflects his diversity in the use of metaphors and varied versification. Gray received the Caribbean Writer Prize for Poetry in 1997.

256.   _____. *Lillian's Songs*. Toronto, Ontario: Lilibel Publications, 1996.

This is Gray's second book of poems. A volume of 60+ poems concerning home, love, protest, and hope.

257.   ____. *The Woolgatherer.* Leeds: Peepal Tree Press, 1994.

This collection of poems is autobiographical in nature. Gray's poetry covers situations that involve his evolution from childhood to manhood. Extensive use of metaphors, rhyme, and rhythm define Gray's style.

258.   Hamilton, Judith. *Rain Carvers*. Kingston: Sandberry Press, 1992.

This collection of 40 poems showcases Hamilton's versatility in moving between Jamaican English and Standard English. The title poem "Rain Carvers" evokes strong imagery of Hamilton's homeland, Jamaica.

259.   Harris, Alan and A.L. Hendriks. *Check*. Headland, 1988.

This volume of poetry is written by two close friends. Poems are prefaced by statements from the poets with the poems that follow serving as responses/answers to the former. A collection of 50+ poems.

260.   Harris, Claire. *Fables From the Women's Quarters*. Toronto: Williams-Wallace, 1984.

In this collection, Harris's linguistic techniques combine to move the reader into a metaphoric space which is crowded with the hopes, fears, aspirations, and experiences of the Caribbean woman.

261.   ____. *The Conception of Winter.* Toronto: Williams-Wallace, 1988.

This collection of poetry by Harris explores movement from birth-home to a new "adult" home and the attendant emotions of such a move. Some of the poems have appeared in literary journals and anthologies.

262.   ____. *Dipped in Shadow*. Fredericton: Goose Lane Editions, 1996.

This collection of five poems of varying lengths examine a range of issues including incest, violence, war, and disease. Her work speaks directly to all women, regardless of color or culture, to combat the vices of society.

263.   ____. *Drawing Down A Daughter*. Fredericton: Goose Lane Editions, 1992.

This is Harris's fifth collection of poems. In this collection of prose poetry, Harris presents a woman who communicates with her unborn daughter through journals, letters, stories, and imaginings about the world of the West Indies and Canada.

264.   _____. *She*. Fredericton: Goose Lane Editions, 2000.

In her seventh book, Harris examines mental illness in women and how it impacts their lives and those of their families. This text is best described as a novel in prose and prose poetry.

265.   _____. *Translation into Fiction*. Fredericton: Goose Lane Editions, 1984.

This collection of poetry is divided into three sections entitled Translation Into Fiction, After the Chinese, and Deformed Angels. Harris's poetry underscores the necessity of having/creating a language capable of expressing the African Caribbean experience. She addresses the English language limitation in expressing "black things" in "white words".

266.   _____. *Travelling To Find A Remedy*. Fredericton: Goose Lane Editions, 1986.

Harris engages in experiments with typography and page arrangement in this collection. This collection is a blend of poems focusing on cultural differences in relationships, parting, and suicide/death.

267.   Harris, Wilson. *Eternity to Season*. London: New Beacon, 1978.

This collection of poems was first published privately in 1954 in Georgetown, British Guiana (now Guyana). Due to a growing demand for Harris's work, this edition was published 24 years after the first printing. Some changes occur in this edition: a short play has been omitted as well as several poems. The appendix carries the work as it appeared in the first printing (to satisfy certain specifications of the publisher, New Beacon).

268.   Hendriks, A. L. *These Green Islands and other poems*. Kingston, Jamaica: Bolivar Press, 1971.

The poems that refer to "these green islands" contain a subtitle to indicate which island is being poeticized. The "other poems" are introspective – reflecting the poet's life and concerns.

269.   _____. *The Islanders and other Poems*. Kingston, Jamaica: Savacou Cooperative, 1983.

This is Hendrik's fifth major collection of poems. His critically acclaimed verse sequence "The Islanders" serves as the title of this collection, which contains 13 other poems.

270.   _____. *Madonna of the Unknown Nation*. London: Workshop Press, 1974.

This volume of poetry represents an introduction, of sorts, of Hendriks to the British reading audience. The poems reflect both his Caribbean heritage and his experiences as a resident in several European cities.

271.   _____. *To Speak Simply: Selected Poems, 1961-1986*. Sutton: Hippopotamus Press, 1988.

This volume consists of poems from two collections – *The Islanders* and *D'ou venons-nous? Que sommes-nous? Ou allons-nous?* Some of the poems are written in Jamaican English (patois). Works are representative of his style in blending elements of the Caribbean and Europe.

272.   Henry, Melchoir. *Dead Country*. Castries: The Source, 1981.

This collection of 20 poems is preceded by a foreword written by the poet Kendel Hippolyte. Hippolyte describes Melchoir's poems as meditations on Caribbean history, which paint a realistic, albeit grim, image of that history.

273.   Hippolyte, Kendel. *Bearings*. St. Lucia: Dunesville Enterprises, 1986.

The opening poem of this volume, "poem in a manger" reveals Hippolyte's poetic philosophy about the function and purposes of writing. The title poem "bearings" addresses the uncertainty attached to a definite sense of time and place.

274.   _____. *Birthright*. Leeds: Peepal Tree Press, 1997.

This is the first collection of poems by Hippolyte published outside of his native St. Lucia. The work combines the best of the oral and literary traditions merging into poems that communicate the range of life's emotions.

275.   _____. *Island in the Sun, Side Two*. St. Lucia: UWI Extra Mural Department, 1980.

The poems in this volume are expressions of protest and love. Hippolyte uses both Caribbean dialect and Standard English in making his poetic messages accessible. A foreword is written by the poet and critic Mervyn Morris.

276.   _____. *The Labyrinth*. Castries: The Source, 1993.

A closeness to home [the Caribbean] mingled with home abroad is reflected in this collection of poems. Some of the poems have appeared in the *Graham House Review* and in the anthologies *Confluence* and *The Heinemann Book of Caribbean Poetry*.

277.   Hopkinson, Abdur-Rahman Slade. *The Friend*. Georgetown, Guyana: Curriculum Development Center, 1976.

This volume is the companion to the volume *The Madwoman of Papine*. Whereas the poems in *Madwoman...* are more secular, those in this volume are more religious in tone and reflect a contemplative individual.

278.   _____. *The Madwoman of Papine*. Georgetown, Guyana, 1976.

In a prefatory note, Hopkinson says that the poems in this volume revolve around an adolescence and manhood lived in the West Indies, Guyana, and the USA. The title poem "The Madwoman of Papine" presents a vivid look at a slice of Jamaican life and the effects of society on the individual psyche.

279.   Itwaru, Arnold. *body rites (beyond the darkening)*. Toronto: TSAR, 1991.

In the frontispiece to this collection, Itwaru speaks to the substance of the poems within as informed by his meditation on both pleasant and unpleasant experiences.

280.   _____. *Entombed Survivals*. Toronto: Williams-Wallace, 1987.

These poems focus on the search for inner peace. Some of the poems have previously appeared in a number of anthologies. Itwaru is the winner of the A.J. Seymour Prize for Poetry and the Guyana History and Art Council's First Prize for Poetry.

281.   _____. *Shattered Songs*. Toronto: Aya Press, 1982.

This slim volume of lyrical poems comments on the position of the society "outsider" as well as on the cultural and historical traditions/conditions of Itwaru's background. The poems reflect vivid images of violence borne out of the author's relationship to his historical past and present life in Canada.

282.   James, Cynthia. *Iere, My Love: A Collection of Poems*. Port of Spain, 1990.

This collection of 50 poems is divided into four sections, each with a cover page entitled "iere, my love." This is James' first collection of poems. Some of the poems were previously published in the *Trinidad Express*.

283.   Johnson, Amryl. *Long Road to Nowhere*. Oxford: Sable Publications, 1982.

This collection of 22 poems contains poems that deal with isolation, oppression, and search for identity. The poet was born in Trinidad and has lived in England since she was eleven.

284.   Johnson, Linton Kwesi. *Dread Beat and Blood*. London: Bogle – L'Ouverture, 1975.

This collection of protest poems is organized into five sections: Down De Road, Time to Explode, Song of Blood, Bass Cultures, and One Love. A brief glossary of terms is at the end of the text. The poems are in both English and German.

285.   _____. *Inglan is a Bitch*. London: Race Today Publications, 1980.

Several of the poems in this collection are set to music and are on the LPs "Dread Beat an' Blood," Forces of Victory," and "Bass Culture." This, Johnson's third collection of verse, reflects the concerns of Blacks, in their diversity, in England. The title poem "Inglan is a Bitch" is a working class hymn to/of the black community.

286.   _____. *Tings An' Times: Selected Poems*. Newcastle upon Tyne: Bloodaxe Books, Ltd., 1991.

The twenty-four poems in this collection have been drawn from various collections and recordings of Johnson: *Voices of the Living Dead, Dread Beat an Blood, Inglan Is A Bitch, Making History,* and the anthologies *Hinterland* and *The Penguin Book of Caribbean Verse.*

287.   _____. *Voices of the Living and the Dead*. London: Race Today Publications, 1988.

This work was first published by *Towards Racial Justice* (now *Race Today*) in 1974. The three poems - "Voices of the Living and the Dead," "Youths of Hope," and "Five Nights of Bleeding" reflect the situations and feelings of Blacks in British society during the summer of 1981.

288.   Kallicharan, Laxhmie. *Hear the Ghungrus Sing*. Georgetown, Guyana: Shraadanjali Publications, 1992.

Kallicharan's poetry presents a vivid look at Indo-Caribbean culture through a variety of cultural situations. While the poems are highly personal, they reach out to embrace many universal concerns of Indo-Caribbeans, specifically, and Caribbeans, generally. A foreword by Rooplall Monar provides background on Kallicharan's poetic style.

289.   Keens-Douglas, Paul. *Is Town Say So*. Port of Spain: Keensdee Productions, 1982.

This is a collection of dialect articles (written for the Trinidad evening paper, *The Sun*) and other stories and poems. The poems (and stories) were developed by Keens-Douglas through continued performance before committing the work to the printed page.

290.   _____. *Lal Shop: Short Stories and Dialect Poetry*. Port of Spain: Keensdee Productions, 1984.

This collection contains articles originally written in dialect for the column "Is Town Say So" in the *Trinidad and Tobago Sunday Express*. Section I contains short stories and Section II contains dialect poems. Keens-Douglas emphasizes dialect as an oral medium for serious as well as humorous dialect.

291.   _____. *Role Call*. Diego Martin, Trinidad: Keensdee Productions, 1997.

This is a volume of poetry and short stories. Notes on the author and a Foreword written by poet and critic Mervyn Morris precedes the poems and stories. A glossary of terms to ease reading of Trinidadian language is provided at the close of the text.

292.   _____. *Tanti at De Oval*. Port of Spain: Keensdee Productions, 1992.

This volume of selected works, mostly poetry, covers work written by Keens-Douglas from 1974-1992. All of these works have previously appeared in other published works by the author.

293.   _____. *Tell Me Again*. Port of Spain: Keensdee Productions, 1979.

This volume of poems represents Keens-Douglas's attempt to combine all the works he has written and performed that have not yet been published. It captures experiences and emotions of a five-year period, 1974-1979.

294.   _____. *Tim Tim*. Port of Spain: Keensdee Productions, 1976.

The poet calls this volume a collection of some of his "lighter pieces of dialect poetry." The introduction, written by Lawrence D. Carrington, provides a discussion of the use of Standard language and dialect.

295.   _____. *When Moon Shine*. Port of Spain: Keensdee Productions, 1975.

This is Keens-Douglas's first published volume of poems. The poems are in dialect and standard English. In the Introduction, Victor Questel comments on the difficulty inherent in critically analyzing a collection of poems written in two forms. The introduction provides (early) insight into Keens-Douglas's poetic techniques.

296.   Kellman, Anthony. *The Broken Sun*. Barbados: Letchworth Press Ltd., 1984.

A collection of twelve poems by Bajan poet, Kellman. In 1973 he was hailed as the most outstanding poet in the National Festival of Creative Arts (NIFCA). He has been lauded by Kamau Brathwaite as "one of the finest new generation Bajan poets..."

297.   _____. *In Depths of Burning Light*. Barbados: Letchworth Press, 1982.

The poems in this collection are divided into three sections: The Crumbling Mountain, Around the Reef, and Burning Light. The works focus on Kellman's theme of power and faith and its omnipresence in people's lives. An introduction to the collection is written by Kamau Brathwaite.

298.   _____. *Watercourse*. Leeds: Peepal Tree Press, 1990.

Introductory comments by Joseph Bruchac and Edouard Glissant focus on Kellman's skill in his use of the Caribbean landscape to speak to an experience in the Caribbean that enables him to adequately express the concerns of the larger world. The poem "Beached" is illustrative of his technique.

299.   King, Jane. *In To the Centre*. St. Lucia, 1990.

Some of these 30+ poems have appeared in *Kyk-over-Al* (Guyana), *Confluence* (St. Lucia), *Creation Fire* (Sister Vision, Trinidad), *Graham House Review* (Colgate University Press, USA), *Caribbean Poetry Now* (Edward Arnold, U. K.) The Fine Arts Scheme gave this collection a Literary Award in 1990.

300.   _____. *Fellow Traveller.* Jamaica: Sandberry Press, 1994.

This collection of poems by King bears witness to her many travels as a young woman and a developing writer. Some of the poems were written at Yaddo, an artists' colony in New York, where she was in residence on a Witter Bynner Fellowship in 1992.

301.   La Rose, John. *Eyelets of Truth Within Me*. London: New Beacon Books, 1992.

This collection of 25 poems presents images of the past – places, persons, and things – in contrast to life in the present. The last poem, "Unending Journey" is dedicated to Kamau Brathwaite.

302.   Lee, John Robert. *Clearing Ground.* Boston: New Life Fellowship, 1991.

The poems in this slim volume emphasize Lee's Christian beliefs. Concerns with truth, honesty, and harmonious living are major themes in his work.

303.   _____. *Dread Season*. St. Lucia, 1978.

This poem, in nine sections, presents clear images of life in St. Lucia. The poetic persona comes to terms with life, which includes death.

304.   _____. *Possessions*. St. Lucia, 1984.

This short collection of three poems is offered in memoriam to Maurice Bishop (Grenadian leader), Mikey Smith (Jamaican poet), and Ermine Volney (St. Lucian teacher), all murdered at an early age. The poems reflect the pain and anguish that come with change and social unrest.

305.   _____. *The Prodigal*. St. Lucia, 1983.

This single poem, in seven sections, uses Chapters 15 and 24 of Luke (The Holy Bible) as the departure point for issues of growth and development.

306.   _____. *Translations*. Castries: Sunshine Bookshop, 1993.

This volume contains new poems as well as poems from the following collections: *Vocations and other poems, Dread Season, The Prodigal, Possessions, Saint Lucian,* and *Clearing Ground.* This collection of 12 poems is dedicated to Derek Walcott.

307.   _____. *Vocation.* St. Lucia: UWI Extra Mural Department, 1975.

Many of the poems in this collection have previously appeared in a number of Caribbean newspapers and journals. A "Prologue to the Poet" highlights the poems in this collection as those which focus on the universal to the intensely personal such as "Fragments to a Return." The text is illustrated by Alwin Bully.

308.   Leonard, Joseph A. *True Confession: Love Poems and Others.* St. Thomas: W.I.M.I.S. Music Publisher, 1990.

This collection of very short poems was written based on Leonard's love and life experiences with a variety of women. A short prose piece, "To Myself," concludes the collection.

309.   Mandiela, Ahdri Zhina. *Dark Diaspora ... in dub.* Toronto: Sister Vision Press, 1995.

This collection of dub poetry is (actually) a theatre piece; the first workshop production was presented at the *Fringe of Toronto 91*. Specifically, the poems encompass 30 years (1960s-1990s) of the Black psyche (in the Diaspora) from a woman's perspective in 1990's Canada.

310.   _____. *Special Rikwes*. Toronto: Sister Vision Press, 1990.

This is Ahdri's first volume of poetry, organized into three chapters: First Dub, Vershan, and Special Riwkes. The poet strives to involve the reader in the poetry by acquainting him/her with sounds and imagery in a progressive manner as the three sections progress. A glossary of Jamaican terms is included to promote accessibility to meaning.

311.   Manley, Rachel. *A Light Left On.* Leeds: Peepal Tree Press, 1992.

This collection of 40 poems cover topics that reflect Manley's background and family lineage in the artistic and political movements in Jamaica.

312.   _____. *Poems 2*. Barbados: Coles Printery, 1978.

The 40 poems in this collection are a combination of reminiscences of the past and concerns with life in the present. The final poem in the collection "And Music Like Upcurling Smoke" is dedicated to George Campbell.

313.   _____. *Prisms*. Kingston, Jamaica: Hyde, Held, and Blackburn, 1972.

This volume contains twenty-eight poems accompanied by illustrations. Poems such as "Fable" and "Death, You Strange Animal" are illustrative of the searching, introspective mood of the poems.

314.   Markham, E. A. *Games and Penalties: A Collection of Poems*. Great Britain: Poet & Printer, 1980.

This volume of 20 poems reflects Markham's life in Montserrat, England, France, Germany, and Sweden in its sweeping inclusion of a variety of concerns and emotions. The closing poem "Words Fit to Eat" examines the function and power/powerlessness of words and writing.

315.   _____. *Human Rites: Selected Poems, 1970-1982*. London: Anvil Press, 1984.

This selection of poems by Markham reflects the range of his writing during a twelve year period. The poems focus on his West Indian heritage and issues revolving around love, history, society, and politics.

316.   _____. *Living in Disguise*. London: Anvil Press, 1986.

This volume of poetry is divided into six sections: Sally Goodman/The Housewife's Revenge (1972-1976); Paul St. Vincent/Lambchops, a Second Helping; The Cost of Living, Part One; On the Redistribution of Wealth; The Cost of Living, Part Two; and Four Letters and a Sermon. Notes (at the end of the volume) provide interesting perspectives on the poems.

317.   _____. *Mad and Other Poems*. Warks: Aquila/The Phaethon Press, 1973.

This is Markham's third book of poetry. The poems, including the title poem, "Mad" are reflections of the poetic persona's life filled with striving toward meaningfulness and clarity.

318.   _____. *Misapprehensions*. London: Anvil Press, 1995.

Markham's sixth collection of poetry reveals a man whose poetic range moves from the comic to the serious. He incorporates a love for his country with a knowledge of his life in various European cities. The volume is divided into eight topical sections.

319.   _____. *Towards the End of a Century*. London: Anvil Press, 1989.

Each of the four sections of this volume of poems is preceded by haiku. The topical areas reflect Markham's growing range of poetic concerns: Towards the End of a Century, Family, Poems for the Occasion, and (Counting the Letters of) Love.

320.   Matthews, Marc. *A Season of Sometimes*. Leeds: Peepal Tree Press, 1992.

Matthews' skill as a sound poet is highlighted in this collection of over twenty-five poems. Notes and a glossary are provided at the end of the collection to clarify oral patois terms.

321.   _____. *Guyana, My Altar*. London: Karnak House, 1987.

In an introduction written by Edward Kamau Brathwaite, "What Marcus Tellin' Us," he emphasizes Matthews' skill as a "sound poet" engaged in *oralography*. Poems are explorations of Guyanese life and culture.

322.   McCallum, Shara. *The Water Between Us*. Pittsburgh: University of Pittsburgh Press, 1999.

The poems in this collection reflect McCallum's Afro-Jamaican and Venezuelan background. The ethos of the Caribbean is captured in her lyrical style which mingles descriptions of the landscape with revelations of the heart.

323.   McDonald, Ian. *Essequibo*. Cornwall: Peterloo Poets, 1992.

Some of the poems in this collection of 30+ first appeared in the journals *Kyk-over-Al, The Caribbean Writer,* and *Poetry Matters*.

324.   _____. *Jaffo the Calypsonian*. Leeds: Peepal Tree, 1994.

This collection of poems reflects McDonald's early work available for the first time in a single volume. The poems have major notes of optimism about the possibilities for Caribbean people.

325.   _____. *Mercy Ward*. Cornwall: Peterloo Poets, 1988.

This is McDonald's first large collection of poems. The poems were written based on the poet's experiences as a visitor in the wards of a hospital for the poor and destitute.

326.   _____. *Selected Poems*. Georgetown, Guyana: The Labour Advocate 1983.

This collection of 25 poems are selections from McDonald's early writing as well as current material. McDonald's work as both poet and novelist is evident in the characters that emerge in his poems and the storylines that develop. A. J. Seymour writes an Introduction to the collection.

327.   McKay, Claude. *The Dialect Poetry of Claude McKay*. 2 vols. in 1. Plainview, NY: Books for Libraries Press, 1972.

This text includes Volume 1: *Songs of Jamaica* and Volume 2: *Constab Ballads*. Both of these volumes were first published individually in 1912. Claude McKay is the first known Jamaican poet to write in dialect. Wayne Cooper writes the preface to this edition.

328.   McKenzie, Earl. *Against Linearity*. Leeds: Peepal Tree Press, 1992.

McKenzie's poems in this collection deal with the social, economic, and political climate(s) of the Caribbean, particularly Jamaica.

329.   McMorris, Mark. *Figures for a Hypothesis (Suite)*. Buffalo, NY: Leave Books, 1995.

This is a collection of seven prose-style poems. A narrative quality informs poems that deal with a range of societal concerns.

330.   McNeill, Anthony. *Chinese Lanterns from the Blue Child*. Leeds: Peepal Tree, 1998.

This collection of poems reflects a very introspective mood by McNeill. In three sections – Poems, Prose Poems, and Language-in-Music – the poet covers a range of personal experiences and emotions.

331.   _____. *Credences at the Altar of Cloud*. Kingston, Jamaica: Institute of Jamaica, 1979.

This collection of 105 poems includes a prefatory note which confirms that what may appear to be "proofreading errors" are actually McNeill's unique writing techniques. Notes about the page layouts can be found at the end of the Table of Contents.

332.   _____. *Reel From "The Life Movie."* Kingston, Jamaica: Savacou Publications, 1975.

This collection of poems contains an introduction written by the poet and playwright, Dennis Scott. It is worth noting that this collection was printed twice by Savacou Publications, in 1972 and in 1975. The earlier version was withdrawn by the author due to errors found after publication, hence the second version is a markedly different volume.

333.   McTair, Dionyse. *Notes Towards An Escape From Death.* London: New Beacon, 1987.

This collection of introspective poems examines the fragility of life and the unknown qualities of death. A collection of 40+ poems.

334.   McWatt, Mark. *Interiors.* Sydney: Dangaroo Press, 1988.

In a Preface, McWatt contends that the volume of poems reflects his relationship/understanding of the Guyanese landscape (the interior) and his relationship/understanding of the "interior" of feelings and emotions. *Interiors* is his first volume of poetry.

335.   _____. *The Language of Eldorado.* Sydney: Dangaroo Press, 1994.

This collection continues the theme of his first volume of poetry (*Interiors*), a concern with the interior of Guyana and the interior of the individual. Each of the five sections is dedicated to writers McWatt admires.

336.   MockYen, Alma. *Potted Versions.* Kingston, 1992.

This collection of poems is divided into three sections: People, Places, and Things. Her concerns range from the individual to the community to the global. A foreword written by Rex Nettleford provides perspectives on MockYen's writing.

337.   Monar, Rooplall. *Koker.* Peepal Tree Press, 1987.

A collection of 20 + poems by Guyanese writer Monar. Jeremy Poynting, in the introduction contends, "no writer has explored more persistently or more consciously the state of being Indo-Caribbean than Rooplall Monar."

338.   Mordecai, Pamela. *De Man: A Performance Poem*. Toronto: Sister Vision Press, 1995.

A performance poem which the author asserts (in the frontispiece) is "an account of the death of Jesus Christ by Naomi, maid to Pilate's wife, and Samuel, a disabled carpenter of Nazareth, to whom Joseph, Jesus's foster father, taught the trade." Photographs by Martin Mordecai.

339.   _____. *Don't Ever Wake a Snake*. Kingston, Jamaica: Sandberry Press, 1991.

This collection contains 9 poems and 2 stories for children. Animals and insects serve as the characters and voices in most of the works.

340.   _____. *Journey Poem*. Kingston, Jamaica: Sandberry Press, 1989.

This collection of 30 + poems contains some early writing previously published in *Arts Review, Bim, Caribbean Quarterly, Jamaica Woman, Nimrod, Jamaica Journal, Savacou, Focus 1983, Pathways,* and *The Penguin Book of Caribbean Verse.*

341.   Morris, Mervyn. *Examination Centre*. London: New Beacon Books, 1992.

Some of the poems in this collection of 40+ have appeared in journals and newspapers such as *Jamaica Journal, The Sunday Gleaner, Bim, Kyk-over-Al, The Times Literary Supplement,*and *Trinidad and Tobago Review,* among others.

342.   _____. *On Holy Week*. Sydney: Dangaroo Press, 1993.

This collection of poems carries the subtitle, "A Sequence of Poems for Radio." Earlier versions of this collection have appeared in *The Daily Gleaner* and *Bim.*

343.   _____. *The Pond*. London: New Beacon Books, 1997.

This volume of poetry was originally published in 1973. This is a revised edition with notes on earlier versions of [some] poems. Four of the poems have new titles in a collection where the inner thoughts of a man alert to the sounds and sights of the world are presented.

344.   _____. *Shadowboxing: Poems*. London: New Beacon Books, 1979.

A collection of 40+ short poems. Some have appeared in the following journals and newspapers: *Ariel, Arts Review, Bim, The Jamaica Daily News, Jamaica Journal, Nimrod, Now, Pepperpot, Public Opinion, The Sunday Gleaner, and Topia.*

345.   Mutabaruka (formerly Allan Hope). *The First Poems, 1970-1979.* Kingston, Jamaica: Paul Issa, 1980.

These poems were all written during the 1970s, a heightened period of Black consciousness in Jamaica. Individual poems are divided into Parts One and Two by the year in which they were written. An introduction by Mervyn Morris provides a brief but informative look at Muta's life, early work, and influences.

346.   _____. *Outcry.* Kingston, Jamaica: Swing Publishers, 1973.

These early poems by Mutabaruka reflect his concern with people arming themselves with knowledge in coming to a greater consciousness of themselves and their environment. The poems reflect Muta's concerns about Jamaica.

347.   Mutabaruka and Faybiene. *Sun and Moon.* 1976.

This dually-authored volume contains 29 poems that have overtones and undertones of militancy coupled with the need for change. The poems are gathered into two sections – Sun and Moon – the title of the book.

348.   Natural, Cherry. *Come Meck We Reason.* Kingston, Jamaica: CARESO/ Volunteers Social Service, 1989.

Cherry Natural is one of the few but growing number of female dub poets from the West Indies. Her poetry is heavily focused on issues that affect women and children. The volume contains poetry, "brain buster" exercises, and find-a-word puzzles. Cherry Natural was born Marcia Wedderburn in Jamaica in 1960.

349.   Nichols, Grace. *The Fat Black Woman's Poems.* London: Virago, 1984.

This collection is divided into three sections: The Fat Black Woman's Poems, In Spite of Ourselves, Back Home Contemplation, and I is a Long Memoried woman. *The Fat Black Woman's Poems* celebrate self despite difference through an emphasis on physical size while covering a full range of social, cultural, and political issues.

350.   _____. *I is a Long Memoried Woman*. London: Karnak House, 1990.

This volume is an exploration through poetry of Black African women's lives as slaves on the sugar plantations of the Caribbean region. Emphasis is placed on the omnipresence of memory in women's lives.

351.   _____. *Lazy Thoughts of a Lazy Woman, and Other Poems*. London: Virago, 1989.

The frontispiece describes this collection as "sensuous, witty, and provocative... poems of laid-back and not-so-laid back musings, sagas and spells ...Caribbean migration...moments of poignancy and loss..."

352   _____. *Sunris*. London: Virago Press, 1996.

In the introduction to this collection, Nichols says that *Sunris* is a poem about "a woman who makes a journey towards self-discovery and self-naming, through carnival." She writes the poems with an emphasis on the art form calypso or 'kaiso'.

353.   Onuora, Oku (formerly Orlando Wong). *Echo*. Kingston, Jamaica: Sangster's, 1977.

This volume of 26 poems reflects Onuora's attitudes on poverty, oppression, and political indifference. Writing in both Jamaican English (patois) and Standard English, some of his best known poems such as "Pressure Drop," "No Poet," and "I Write About" are included.

354.   Persaud, Sasenarine. *Between the Dash and the Comma*. Leeds: Peepal Tree Press, 1991.

This is Persaud's second collection of poems. His work reflects his Indo-Caribbean background as he explores the range of emotions and experiences of East Indians from the Caribbean and South America.

355.   _____. *Demerary Telepathy*. Leeds: Peepal Tree Press, 1988.

A collection of poems which emphasize the Indo-Caribbean people's placement/grounding in the Caribbean region. The poem, "The West Indian" highlights the historical, cultural, social, and political division among Caribbeans of Indian and African descent. This is Persaud's first collection of poems.

356.   _____. *A Surf of Sparrow's Songs*. Toronto: TSAR, 1996.

In this collection of poetry, Persaud moves the reader between Miami and Toronto in a series of poems concerned with love and interwoven with his Indo-Caribbean heritage.

357.   Philip, Geoffrey. *Exodus and Other Poems*. St. Croix: The Caribbean Writer, 1990.

This volume of poems by Jamaican born Philip reflects his memories and love for his country. The twenty-one poems touch on life in Jamaica and his current life in Miami, Florida.

358.   _____. *Florida Bound*. Leeds: Peepal Tree Press, 1995.

Philip combines Jamaican Creole language and Standard English in this collection. While the poems express his regret over feeling forced to leave Jamaica for a better life in Miami, Florida, Philip manages to infuse the poetry with positive notes in his reflections on his new life in the USA.

359.   Philip, Marlene Nourbese. *Looking for Livingstone: An Odyssey of Silence*. Stratford: Mercury Press, 1991.

This novel in poetry and prose revolves around a woman traveling alone through Africa in search of Dr. David Livingstone, the "recognized discoverer" of Africa. Philip examines the silence of indigenous peoples in a story of parables, suspense, and dreams.

360.   _____. *Salmon Courage*. Toronto: Williams-Wallace, 1983.

This slim volume of 23 poems are mini-portraits of Philip's views on love, family, tradition, change, and, above all, courage. The title poem "Salmon Courage" presents an inside look at the poet's life.

361.   _____. *She Tries Her Tongue, Her Silence Softly Breaks*. London: The Women's Press, 1993.

This volume of poetry was the winner of the Casa de las Americas Prize 1988. The poems cover concerns with language, colonialism, exile, and racism from a Black woman's point of view. An Afterword entitled "The Absence of Writing or How I Became a Spy" provides an insight into her writing technique.

362.   _____. *Thorns*. Toronto: Williams-Wallace, 1980.

This is Philips's first published volume of poetry. These early poems reflect life in her birth-home, Trinidad-Tobago, and her life in Jamaica. A glossary of Caribbean and African words used in the poems is included at the close of the text.

363.   Pollard, Velma. *Crown Point and Other Poems*. Leeds: Peepal Tree Press, 1988.

This is the first volume of poems by Pollard, a Jamaican who lectures in Education at the University of the West Indies (Kingston). Some poems in this collection have been published in *Bim*, *Caribbean Quarterly*, *Jamaica Journal*, and *Jamaica Woman*.

364.   _____. *Shame Trees Don't Grow Here...but poincianas bloom*. Leeds: Peepal Tree Press, 1992.

This collection of poems opens with a mini-essay on the changing face of the British Empire as seen through the poet's eyes while at Heathrow Airport.

365.   Polydere, Kay. *Pause to Ponder: Poems and Calypsoes*. Roseau, Dominica, 1992.

This collection is divided into two sections: poems and (three) calypsoes. Explanatory notes are included at the end of the text.

366.   _____. *Issues and Opinions*. Roseau, Dominica, 1997.

Polydore explores a full range of concerns, domestic and otherwise of Dominican women, specifically, and Dominican people, generally.

367.   _____. *For Mirth and Meditation: Poems and Songs*. Roseau, Dominica, 1993.

This collection follows the structure of Polydore's 1992 collection with poems and songs (calypsoes) and explanatory notes at the end of the text.

368.   Questel, Victor D. *Hard Stares*. Trinidad: New Voices, 1979.

This is Questel's (1949-1982) last book of poetry. In an in-depth introduction by Gordon Rohlehr (his friend, tutor, and colleague at UWI/ Trinidad), the reader has access to some of Questel's major themes. Divided into four parts: Looking, The Glare Hurts, The Eye Explodes, and Cast A Cold Eye.

369.   _____. *Near Mourning Ground*. Trinidad: The New Voices, 1979.

The poems in this collection reflect Questel's questions and tentative answers to the changes in the Caribbean. His poems have rhythms that appear influenced by the calypsos of his home, Trinidad.

370.   Rahim, Jennifer. *Mothers Are Not the Only Linguists and Other Poems*. Trinidad: The New Voices, 1992.

In her first book of poems, Rahim searches for words/language to adequately express her life as a woman (first), citizen, and human being. An introduction written by Margaret Watts provides background about Rahim's writing techniques and her subject matter.

371.   Rankine, Claudia. *The End of the Alphabet*. New York: Grove Press, 1998.

This is Rankine's latest collection of poems. Some works have appeared in the following journals: *Boston Review, The Marlboro Review, The Mississippi Review, PEQUOD,* and *The Southern Review*. The volume contains twelve poems.

372.   _____. *Nothing in Nature is Private*. Cleveland: The Cleveland Poetry Center, 1994.

This volume of poems by Jamaican native Rankine marks the 100th book published by The Cleveland Poetry Center as part of its International Poetry Competition. Rankine's work was the 1993 First Place Winner.

373.   Roach, E. M. *The Flowering Rock: Collected Poems, 1938-1974*. Leeds: Peepal Tree Press, 1992.

A foreword by Ian McDonald and an introduction by Kenneth Ramchand highlight the importance of this collection of E. M. Roach's poems. Organized in two sections: Published Poems 1938-1973 and Unpublished Poems.

374.   Roopnaraine, Rupert. *Suite for Supriya*. Leeds: Peepal Tree Press, 1993.

This collection of short verse is organized into sections entitled: Poems of Engagement, Poems of Idolatry, Recoveries, Divertimiento, and Envoi.

375.   _____. *Web of October*. Leeds: Peepal Tree Press, 1988.

This collection of poems was written by Roopnaraine in the spaces of the critically exploratory essay [Rereading Martin Carter] "You Are Involved," on Martin Carter's artistry and impact of his collection *Poems of Resistance*.

376. Roy, Lucinda. *Wailing the Dead to Slee*p. London: Bogle L'Ouverture, 1988.

This is Roy's first collection of published poetry. Her poems cover childhood, sex, love, and death in a looking backward and moving forward. An introduction to the volume is written by Nikki Giovanni.

377. Royes, Heather. *The Caribbean Raj*. Kingston, Jamaica: Ian Randle Publishers, 1996.

This is Royes' first collection of poetry. The book is divided into four sections: The Caribbean Raj, Songs of the 70s', Personal Songs, and Halycon Days. The first two sections deal with the social and political milieu of Jamaica with the last two sections more personal and based on the impact of social and political conditions on the individual.

378. St. John, Bruce. *Bumbatuk I*. Barbados: Cedar Press, 1982.

This is St. John's second book of poems written in Barbadian dialect. The poems are organized into two sections: A Song Cycle (Part I. The Foetus – Pains and Part II. The Foetus) and We Country. His poems represent the Barbadian folk (oral) tradition, its values, and concerns.

379. _____. *Joyce and Eros and Varia*. Barbados: Yoruba Press, 1976.

This volume represents St. John's first book written in Standard English. His first poems were written in the English Creole of Barbados. The poems are gathered in three sections: Varia – Higher Learning, Varia – The Caribbean, and Joyce and Eros.

380. Salkey, Andrew. *Jamaica*. Hutchinson & Co., Ltd., 1973.

This long poem is divided into four parts: Caribbea, Slavery to Liberation, Mento Time, and Caribbean Petchary. The focus of the poem is Jamaica's slave trade, colonization, and the ensuing struggle for identity and freedom of Caribbean peoples.

381.   Scott, Dennis. *Dreadwalk*. London: New Beacon Books, Ltd., 1982.

The poems in this collection move between Standard English and Creole with a strong acknowledgement of the Rastafarian values of community as well as individuality.

382.   _____. *Strategies*. Kingston, Jamaica: Sandberry Press, 1989.

This collection is framed by the poems "Harboursong" and Journeysong" which speak to the experiences of many Caribbeans living outside of their home country.

383.   _____. *Uncle Time*. University of Pittsburgh Press, 1973.

This early collection of poems by Scott was an International Poetry Forum selection and won the 1974 Commonwealth Poetry Prize for the best collection published in the British Commonwealth in the preceding year.

384.   Sekou, Lasana M. *Born Here*. St. Maarten: House of Nehesi, 1986.

In this collection of nationalistic poetry, Sekou explores and examines the world of the Caribbean and specifically that of St. Maarten/St. Martin. Poems of revolution, love, and new beginnings are divided into three sections: born here, love majesty, and Caribbean times.

385.   _____. *Mother Nation*. St. Maarten: House of Nehesi, 1991.

In a commentary written by Armando Lampe, Sekou is called a "voice in the desert of his Caribbean island, St. Martin (North and South)." His collection is organized into sections entitled: Pelican Song, Fetish Dance, Caribbean Journey, and Kitchen Notes.

386.   _____. *Nativity & Dramatic Monologues*. St. Maarten: House of Nehesi, 1988.

This volume contains the epical poem "Nativity," which is concerned with the building and development of the Caribbean – a pan-Caribbean. The five dramatic monologues reflect St. Maarten/St. Martin in historical, political, and social aspects.

387.   _____. *Quimbe: Poetics of Sound*. St. Maarten: House of Nehesi, 1991.

The poems in this collection appear rhythmical and impromptu like the title, *Quimbe* (impromptu, topical St. Maarten song sung without musical accompaniment). Poems are organized into three sections: home, garden balsam, and cross culturing.

388.   Senior, Olive. *Gardening in the Tropics*. Toronto: McClelland and Stewart, 1994.

Senior paints vivid word-pictures of the Caribbean in her second book of poetry. Her work is accessible in her use of everyday images, language, and experiences of the Caribbean and its people.

389.   _____. *Talking of Trees*. Kingston: Calabash Publications, 1985.

This collection of poems blends the themes of ancestry, history, culture, and rural and urban landscapes/living conditions. Senior brings together a number of elements into a unique whole as she creates poems that present the individual as an amalgamation of attitudes, philosphies, and mores.

390.   Seymour, A. J. *Images of Majority*. Georgetown, Guyana: Labour Advocate Printery, 1978.

The poems in this collection were written over a ten year period. In an Introduction, Seymour explains approximately seven groupings that his poems fit into. He also discusses his philosophical views about poetry and the importance of Christianity in his writing.

391.   Sharma, P. D. *The New Caribbean Man*. California: Carib House, 1981.

This is Sharma's first book-form publication. The volume is divided into three sections – Deluge, Roots, and Flight, which reflect his Guyanese roots as well as his life in the USA. An introduction written by John Thieme provides a brief overview of his writing style and influences.

392.   Smith, Michael. *It A Come*. Ed. Mervyn Morris. San Francisco: City Lights Books, 1989.

This collection of poems by Smith is edited by Mervyn Morris. In a brief but illuminating introduction, Morris discusses Smith's development as a writer with an emphasis on his methodical approach to his craft.

393.   Stewart, Bob. *Cane Cut*. Kingston: Savacou Cooperative, 1988.

This slim volume of fifteen poems presents a view into various aspects of Jamaican life from the early times ("Christopher Columbus") to the present ("Words Is Not Enough/For Mikey, 1954-1983"). Brief notes on some of the poems follow.

394.   Taylor, Mervyn. *An Island of His Own.* New York and Tucson, AZ: Junction, 1992.

This is Taylor's first published collection of poetry. Some of the poems previously appeared in *Stepping Stones, Antillea, The Caribbean Literary Review, Pivot,* and the anthology *Giant Talk.* The poems reflect his close observation of his surroundings – human and non-human.

395.   Thomas, Elean. *Word Rhythms From the Life of A Woman.* London: Karia Press, 1986.

The work in this collection of poems and short stories reflect the passion of Elean Thomas, a writer and political activist in Jamaica. Thomas' emphasis rests largely with societal issues facing women.

396.   Thompson, Ralph. *The Denting of a Wave.* Leeds: Peepal Tree Press, 1992.

This collection of 48 poems reflects Thompson's Jamaican heritage with a synthesis of his travels abroad. His work has been published in several journals, among them the *London Magazine.*

397.   _____. *Moving On.* Leeds: Peepal Tree Press, 1998.

The poems in this collection reflect a life greatly altered by changes from childhood to the present. Notable is the long poem, "Goodbye Aristotle, So Long America."

398.   Vaughn, H. A. *Sandy Lane and Other Poems.* Bridgetown: Bim, 1985.

This is the second edition of a slim volume of poems written by Vaughan and published 40 years ago (1945). John Wickham, in the introduction, offers this second edition as the work of a "true Barbadian artist.

399.   Walcott, Derek. *Another Life.* New York: Farrar, Straus, and Giroux, 1973.

This autobiographical poem showcases Walcott's connectedness and love to and for St. Lucia and its people. While the poem is about a personal journey, it encompasses the movement from island home to various places in the Caribbean Diaspora – an experience common to many from the Caribbean Basin Region. An Introduction by Robert Hamner provides an analysis of themes, imagery, characters, and structure. A chronology and selected bibliography complete the text.

400. _____. *The Arkansas Testament*. New York: Farrar, Straus and Giroux, 1987.

The thirty-nine poems in this collection are grouped under the headings "Here" and "Elsewhere." The "plot" for this poem is set with the poet checking into a hotel in Fayetteville, Arkansas. While nothing happens physically, the metaphysical occurrences move this work from beginning to end. The poem "The Arkansas Testament," dedicated to Michael Harper, completes the text – a provoking exposé of an African-Caribbean's perception of an African-American's reality.

401. _____. *The Bounty*. New York: Farrar, Straus and Giroux, 1997.

This collection is divided into two sections. The first section, Bounty, is further divided into seven poems/sections. The second section is numbered with some sections bearing the names Signs, Thanksgiving, Parang, Homecoming, Spain, Six Fictions, Italian Eclogues, and A Santa Cruz Quartet.

402. _____. *Collected Poems: 1948-1984*. New York: Farrar, Straus and Giroux, 1986.

An overview of Walcott's major poems from his published collections dating back to 1962: *In A Green Night (1962), Selected Poems (1964), The Castaway and Other Poems (1965), The Gulf (1970), The Gulf and Other Poems (1969), Another Life (1973), Sea Grapes (1976), The Star-Apple Kingdom (1979), The Fortunate Traveller (1981),* and *Midsummer (1984)*.

403. _____. *The Fortunate Traveller*. New York: Farrar, Straus and Giroux, 1981.

The poems in this collection begin in the [section] "North" move to the "South" and return to the "North." The final section contains the title poem, "The Fortunate Traveller" written for Susan Sontag.

404. _____. *Midsummer*. New York: Farrar, Straus and Giroux, 1984.

An index of first lines completes this collection of poetry organized in two parts. The poem "Tropic Zone" is in this collection.

405. _____. *Omeros*. New York: Farrar, Straus and Giroux, 1990.

Walcott creates an epic poem using Homer's epic about Odysseus as the foundation. The title of the work, *Omeros*, bears the Greek name of Homer. Written on a Homeric scale, the poem evokes sorrow, pain, passion, and triumph.

406. _____. *Sea Grapes*. New York: Farrar, Straus and Giroux, 1976.

Classical and Caribbean elements and themes mingle in this early collection of poems by Walcott. Notable is the poem "Names" written for [Edward] Kamau Brathwaite.

407. _____. *Selected Poetry*. Ed. Wayne Brown. London: Heinemann, 1981.

Wayne Brown explains his selections of Walcott's poetry [for the collection] in the Introduction. In addition to organizing the poems in the order of their publication, Brown also has notes (to each of the poems) at the end of the text. A useful text for readers making their first approach to Walcott's work.

408. _____. *The Star-Apple Kingdom*. New York: Farrar, Straus and Giroux, 1979.

A collection of ten poems which explores issues of beginning and continuity of place and self. The title poem closes the collection with a reflection on what was in relationship to that which will/may be.

409. _____. *Tiepolo's Hound*. Farrar, Straus and Giroux, 2000.

This 166 page collection is Walcott's latest collection of poetry. A lifetime of places, experiences, and memories are reflected in these poems. These word reflections are complemented by visual art courtesy of Seth Rubin, New York; Chester Williams, St. Lucia; and Cyan Studios, Trinidad.

410. Wallace, Susan. *Bahamian Scene*. Philadelphia, Pa: Dorrance and Co., 1970.

This is Wallace's first book of poems. In an Introduction, Wallace contends that she wrote these poems in an effort to preserve fading aspects of Bahamian culture. Most of the poems are written in Bahamian dialect.

411. _____. *Island Echoes*. Basingstoke and London: MacMillan Education Ltd., 1973.

This is Wallace's second collection of poems. Unlike her first collection *Bahamian Scene* (written in Bahamian dialect), Wallace writes the poems in this collection in Standard English.

412. Watson, Edward A. *Out of the Silent Stone and Other Poems*. Red Hills, Jamaica: Bruckings Publishing House, 1976.

This collection of 27 poems is reflective of the poet's Jamaican birth, as well as his experiences in other countries. The centrality of the creative process in life is emphasized in his poems about John Coltrane, Miles Davis, and Ezra Pound.

413. Watts, Margaret. *Chautauqua To Chaguanas*. Trinidad & Tobago: Paria Publishing Company Ltd., 1989.

This volume of poems charts Watts' movement from Chautauqua to Chaguanas. Watts was born in Warren, Pennsylvania and has spent time at her parents' cottage, a place of refuge, in Chautauqua, New York. Her husband was born at Chaguanas in Trinidad and Tobago where she first stayed in Trinidad; they now live in Port of Spain.

414. Williams, Clive X. *The Wings of Love and Time*. Frederiksted: Eastern Caribbean Institute, 1990.

This volume of 35 poems focuses on issues of love – romantic, family, and platonic. Williams also addresses the social ills in society such as drugs, child abuse, and violence. The poet grew up in St. Croix.

415. Williams, Milton Vishnu. *Years of Fighting Exile*. Leeds: Peepal Tree Press, 1986.

An introduction by Jeremy Poynting highlights Milton Williams' poetry as reflective of his three "cultural heritages" – African, Indian, and British. Poems centered on love, imagination, and religious experience fill this collection.

416. Zephaniah, Benjamin. *City Psalms*. Newcastle upon Tyne: Bloodaxe Books, 1992.

This is Rasta poet Zephaniah's fourth book of poems. His poetry, a synthesis of rants, rap, ballads, and urban messages, incorporates imagery and concerns of Jamaica and England. Zephaniah's work is best known through his performances and his recordings.

417. _____. *The Dread Affair*. London: Arrow Books, 1985.

This is a collection of 31 poems written at various times in Zephaniah's career. The poems range from those expressing rage, humour, passion, and uncertainty. Zephaniah is one of Britain's most popular performance poets.

418.   _____. *Propa Propaganda*. Newcastle upon Tyne: Bloodaxe Books, 1996.

This volume of poems reflects Zephaniah's growth in oral and performance art and its translation to the printed page. This collection of 51 poems explores a full range of social and political issues with an emphasis on his Rastafarian beliefs.

419.   _____. *Talking Turkeys*. London: Puffin Books, 1994.

This volume of poems is written for children. The 50 poems are contemporary and kid-friendly. Zephaniah divides the collections into three sections: Turkey Talk, Poems From The Last Person On Earth, and More Turkey Talk.

V. *Criticism: Casebooks, Journal Essays and Monographs*

A. Author and Text

420. Asein, Samuel Omo. "Symbol and Meaning in the Poetry of Edward Brathwaite." *World Literature Written in English* 20.1 (Spring 1981): 96-104.

This is an early critical analysis of symbols in Brathwaite's poetry from the 1970s to the 1980s. The essay begins with a brief discussion of the opinions of other critics [such as Mervyn Morris, Damian Grant, and C. L. R. James] on Brathwaite's early work.

421. Baugh, Edward. *Derek Walcott – Memory As Vision: Another Life.* London: Longman Group Ltd., 1978.

An early critical analysis of Walcott's work, *Another Life,* and his major influences. A select bibliography is provided which sheds light on the early range of Walcott's work and attendant criticism.

422. _____. "Goodison on the Road to Heartease." *Journal of West Indian Literature* 1.1 (1986): 13-22.

Baugh discusses Lorna Goodison's development as a poet through an analysis of her poems up to and including the collection *Heartease*. Emphasis is placed on her desire [as poet] to speak for the people.

423.   _____. "Metaphor and Plainness in the Poetry of Derek Walcott." *Literary Half-Yearly* 11.2 (1970): 47-58.

Baugh provides an in-depth discussion of Walcott's use of metaphor in his early poetry. He examines Walcott's development in the use of metaphor and some of his unique qualities as a poet.

424.   _____. "Poetry as Ritual: Reading Kamau Brathwaite." *Journal of West Indian Literature* 8.1 (1998): 1-9.

This essay finds Baugh reevaluating his earlier critical position (in 1967 and 1968) on Brathwaite's *Rights of Passage* and *Masks* as a work of more "pattern than pith." After a reading by Brathwaite at the University of the West Indies (Mona Campus) in 1995, Baugh revisits his comments [and those of other critics] and contends that the "pith is in the pattern, the theme in the form."

425.   _____. "Ripening with Walcott." *Critical Perspectives on Derek Walcott*. Ed. Robert D. Hamner. Washington, DC: Three Continents, 1993. 278-85

This essay examines what Baugh contends is the ideal which governs all of Walcott's work – the cycle of growth. Poems from *Another Life, In A Green Night, The Castaway*, and *Sea Grapes* are used to support this thesis.

426.   Binder, Wolfgang. "David Dabydeen." *Journal of West Indian Literature* 3.2 (1989): 67-80.

This interview provides background on Dabydeen's Guyanese background and his major works to date.

427.   Bobb, June D. *Beating A Restless Drum: The Poetics of Kamau Brathwaite and Derek Walcott*. New Jersey: Africa World Press, 1998.

This text is an examination of the ways that Brathwaite and Walcott configure history and mythology in connecting the past with the present. This text focuses on the theory and practice of both poets.

428. Bodunde, Charles A. "The Black Writer in the Multicultural Caribbean: The Vision of Africa in Edward Kamau Brathwaite's *The Arrivants*." *Matatu: Journal for African Culture and Society* 12 (1994): 17-33.

This essay examines Brathwaite's incorporation of the African world in his poetry about the Caribbean experience. Specifically, Bodunde analyzes the African-Caribbean experience as presented in Brathwaite's *The Arrivants – Rights of Passage, Masks, and Islands*.

429. Breslin, Paul. "I Met History Once, But He Ain't Recognize Me: The Poetry of Derek Walcott." *Triquarterly* (1987): 168-83.

Breslin, in his response to the lack of sustained criticism on Walcott, attempts an in-depth analysis of Walcott's work, specifically *Collected Poems (1948-1984)*. Breslin covers the major themes in Walcott's poetry, including alienation and creolization.

430. Brown, Lloyd W. "Caribbean Castaway New World Odyssey: Derek Walcott's Poetry." *Journal of Commonwealth Literature* 11.2 (1976): 149-59.

This essay focuses on Walcott's poetry that reflects interest in the New World experience (the United States, specifically) with an emphasis on maintaining a Caribbean consciousness.

431. _____. "The Guyanese Voice in West Indian Poetry: A Review of Arthur J. Seymour." *World Literature Written in English* 15 (1976): 246-52.

Seymour's role in contemporary West Indian Poetry is analyzed from the standpoint of his role as both editor of *Kyk-over-Al* and poet-publisher. Brown analyzes the ways in which Seymour functions as a poet of individual concerns as well as a poet of the people.

432. Brown, Stewart. "All Are Involved: The Poetry and Politics of Martin Carter." *New Literature Review* 7 (1979): 66-72.

Brown provides a sweeping, albeit brief, analysis of Carter's poetic artistry. He contends that Carter's volume of poetry, *Poems of Succession*, enable him (and others) to view the scope of Carter's work in a holistic manner for the first time.

433.   _____, ed. *The Art of Derek Walcott*. Seren Books/Dufour Editions, 1991.

Includes a bibliographic reference and index, this is a compilation of Walcott criticism and interpretation. An introduction by Stewart Brown is followed by twelve essays written by a range of scholars, critics, and poets such as Edward Baugh, Mervyn Morris, Fred D'Aguiar, Nana Wilson-Tagoe, Laurence Breiner and others.

434.   _____, ed. *The Art of Kamau Brathwaite*. Wales: Poetry Wales Press Ltd., 1995.

This is a casebook of twelve essays and one interview on Brathwaite's creativity. Select bibliography of Brathwaite included as well as biographical notes on the contributors.

435.   _____. "Walcott's *Fortunate Traveller:* A Patriot in Exile." *Carib* 5 (1989): 1-18.

Using *Fortunate Traveller* as a foundation, Brown explores Walcott's dually self-imposed role as poet and patriot. He examines the pervasive accusation of some critics (and other poets) of Walcott as overly Eurocentric in his writing and views.

436.   Bucknor, Michael Andrew. "Body-Vibes: (S)pacing the Performance in Lillian Allen's Dub Poetry." *Thamyris* 5.2 (1998): 301-22.

This analysis of the Jamaican/Canadian Lillian Allen comes from a materialist critical approach. Bucknor's emphasis rests on the importance of verbal rhythm (rather than verbal reference), process (rather than content), and textual material (rather than textual referentiality). Allen's poetry is interpreted based on "body-memory poetics."

437.   Carr, Brenda. "Come mek wi work together: Community Witness and Social Agency in Lillian Allen's Dub Poetry." *Ariel* 29.3 (July 98): 7-40.

In an exploratory essay, Carr examines the ways in which Allen serves as a cultural griot (in the African tradition) as well as a catalyst for social and political change. A discussion of Allen's complex use of body, rhythm, voice, and "noise" is undertaken by Carr.

438.   Chamberlin, Edward. "Myself Made Otherwise: Edward Kamau Brathwaite's *X/Self*." *Carib* 5 (1989): 19-32.

Chamberlin analyzes *X/Self* as an autobiographical poem, one that deals with the logic of beginnings and a logic of endings. He concludes that Brathwaite offers the reader an account of an expanded sense of selfhood in *X/Self.*

439.   Chang, Victor, ed. *Three Caribbean Poets on Their Work – E. Kamau Brathwaite, Mervyn Morris, and Lorna Goodison.* Mona, Jamaica: University of the West Indies, Institute of Caribbean Studies, 1993.

The three published "lecture-discussions" with Brathwaite, Morris, and Goodison grew out of the Caribbean Seminar Series in late 1985 and early 1986 entitled *Voices In Caribbean Literature.* A number of poets and novelists – Kamau Brathwaite, Mervyn Morris, John Figueroa, Louise Bennett, Olive Senior, Lorna Goodison, Christine Craig, and Vic Reid – participated in the writers' segment of the series (which also included a drama segment). Writers discuss their life and read from their work.

440.   Clarke, George Elliott. "Harris, Philip, Brand: Three Authors in Search of Literate Criticism." *Journal of Canadian Studies* 35.1 (Spring 2000): 161-89.

This essay surveys recent criticism of the writing of three Trinidadian-Canadian women – Claire Harris, M. Nourbese Philip, and Dionne Brand. Clarke contends that contemporary readings of their work are still too traditional and that their work is too often mistakenly labeled as "liberal" social work.

441.   Ciocia, Stefania. "To Hell and Back: The Katabasis and the Impossibility of Epic in Derek Walcott's *Omeros*." *The Journal of Commonwealth Literature* 35.2 (2000): 87-103.

Ciocia takes on the recent debate over Walcott paying homage to Homer in his epic length work, *Omeros.* While some critics argue that Homer's work is inappropriate in depicting Caribbean realities, Ciocia contends that Walcott's use of the trip to the underworld (the katabatic motif) simultaneously suggests originality (in the St. Lucien setting) and reproduction of the classic Homeric epic.

442.   Collymore, Frank. "An Introduction to the Poetry of Derek Walcott." *Savacou: A Journal of the Caribbean Artists Movement* 7-8 (1973): 50-57.

This is the transcript of a very early talk given by critic and publisher Frank Collymore on the poetry of Derek Walcott. An introduction to Walcott's poetry is given through an analysis of some poems from the collection *25 Poems.*

443.   Cooper, Carolyn. "Noh Lickle Twang: An Introduction to the Poetry of Louise Bennett." *World Literature Written in English* 17 (1978): 317-328.

Cooper addresses three areas in this essay: 1) the major currents of 20th century Caribbean poetry in English 2) an evaluation of Bennett's poetry with relationship to these major currents and 3) an identification of significant themes in Bennett's poetry.

444.   _____. "Proverb as Metaphor in the Poetry of Louise Bennett." *Jamaica Journal* 17.2 (1984): 21-24.

This essay focuses on Bennett's use of the Jamaican proverb in her poetry. This focus places emphasis on her skill as an oral and scribal poet, which has been largely ignored by critics until the latter part of the 20th century.

445.   _____. "That Cunny Jamma Oman: The Female Sensibility in the Poetry of Louise Bennett." *Jamaica Journal* 18.4 (November 1985-January 1986): 2-9.

Cooper explores the centrality of the female in Louise Bennett's poetry. The essay examines the female as powerful through "cunning" by focusing on Jamaican female behaviors in the areas of male-female relations, mother and child relations, women and work, and women and politics.

446.   _____. "Words Unbroken By the Beat: The Performance Poetry of Jean Binta Breeze and Mikey Smith." *Wasafiri* 11 (1990): 7-13.

The poetry of Breeze and Smith is discussed based on the interdependent relationship of performer, word, audience, and occasion. Cooper contends that their work moves beyond that of the "ordinary" dub poet whose work frequently becomes dubbed out due to the predominance of the beat.

447.   Cooper, Wayne F. *Claude McKay: Rebel Sojourner in the Harlem Renaissance, A Biography*. Baton Rouge, Louisiana: Louisiana State University, 1987.

This is a well-researched and authoritative biography of the West Indian writer, Claude McKay. His literary fame is explained as predicated largely upon his influence in the Harlem Renaissance literary movement. The first two chapters focus on his Caribbean heritage: Chapter 1 – The Jamaican Family Background and Chapter 2 – The Jamaican Poetry As Autobiography: Claude McKay in 1912.

448.   Dabydeen, David. "On Writing 'Slave Song.'" *Commonwealth Essays and Studies* 8.2 (1986): 46-8.

This is a short essay on Dabydeen's development of his collection *Slave Song*. He discusses the linguistic "vulgarity" of Creole language in its ability to relate the sheer intensity of the (historical) Indo-Caribbean experience.

449.   Diaz, Arturo Maldonado. "Place and Nature in George Lamming's Poetry." *Revista/Review Interamericana* 4 (1974): 402-10.

This essay explores the centrality of place and nature in the early poetry of George Lamming. Diaz comments on the importance of place and nature for West Indians as they move to northern, mostly white-populated cities.

450.   Dove, Rita. "Either I'm Nobody or I'm A Nation." *Parnassus: Poetry in Review* 14.1 (1987): 49-76.

Dove provides a retrospective view of Walcott's work following the publication of his *Collected Poems (1948-1984)*. Dove covers his early work along with his emphasis on nature, history, and the use of visual consciousness in his work.

451.   Fabre, Michel. "Adam's Task of Giving Things Their Name." *New Letters: A Magazine of Fine Writing* 41.1 (1974): 91-107.

Fabre discusses the excessive emphasis that is placed on Walcott's writing along classical guidelines. This essay emphasizes Walcott's development as not only classical but one that embodies the reality of the Caribbean folk tradition.

452.   _____. "The Poetical Journey of Derek Walcott." *Commonwealth Literature and the Modern World*. Ed. Hena Maes-Jelinek. Brussels: Revue Des Langues Vivantes, 1975. 61-68.

Fabre analyzes Walcott's *Another Life* in terms of what it means to be a Caribbean writer. He contends that this work showcases concepts, themes, and images that will inform Walcott's poetry and illuminate the condition of the Caribbean artist and his tradition. Paper presented at a conference on Commonwealth literature at the University of Liege from April 2-5, 1974.

453.   Figueroa, John. "A Note on Derek Walcott's Concern with Nothing."
        Revista/Review Interamericana 4 (1974): 422-28.

        This "note" on Walcott's concern and use of "nothing/nothingness" in
        his poetry comes out of a much longer study by Figueroa on this issue.
        Works from *In A Green Light* (1942) up to *Another Life* (1973) form the
        foundation for this study.

454.   _____. "Omeros." *The Art of Derek Walcott.* Ed. Stewart Brown. Chester
        Springs, PA: Dufour, 1991. 193-213.

        The epic poem *Omeros* is analyzed in four sections, which Figueroa says
        are "well-tried or old fashioned": Historical, Metaphorical, Moral, and
        Anagogical.

455.   Fleming, Carol B. "The Plays and the Poems of Derek Walcott: Singing
        the True Caribbean." *Americas* 34.3 (1982): 8-11.

        Fleming gives a brief view of Walcott's poetry and plays. Fleming's
        analysis concentrates on Walcott's use of the nature metaphor to convey
        "the emotional landscape" of the Caribbean.

456.   Fokkema, Aleid. "On the (False) Idea of Exile: Derek Walcott and Grace
        Nichols." *(Un)Writing Empire.* Ed. Theo D'haen. Amsterdam: Rodopi,
        1998. 99-113.

        This essay considers the work of the well-known Walcott and lesser known
        Nichols beyond that of post-colonial discourse. By examining the manner
        in which each deals with home and identity in their writing, Fokhema
        discusses their work in two of the dominant modes of the twentieth
        century – modernism and post-modernism.

457.   Fox, Robert Elliot. "Derek Walcott: History As Dis-ease." *World
        Literature Written in English* 19 (1980): 62-74.

        Fox examines Walcott's synthesis of standard English, dialect English,
        and French in his poetry. He contends that Walcott's mastery at this
        synthesis enables him to convey the West Indian sensibility thus
        providing a panacea for the "dis-ease" of history.

458.   Fraser, Robert.   *Edward Brathwaite's "Masks": A Critical View.*
        London: Collins, 1981.

This 40 page compilation presents a critical view of Brathwaite's *Masks*, part of the trilogy *The Arrivants*. The sections of the monograph are: I. Edward Brathwaite: Life and Work ; II. Critical View on *Masks* (The trilogy, Migration, Quest, Encounter, The poet's craft, and Lyric and dialogue); III. Brathwaite on language and culture in Africa and the Caribbean; IV. Some critics and commentators; V. Brathwaite in the classroom; VI. Select reading list; and VII. Teaching aids and materials.

459.   Godard, Barbara. "Marlene Nourbese Philip's Hyphenated Tongue or Writing the Caribbean Demotic Between Africa and Arctic." *Major Minorities: English Literatures in Transit.* Amsterdam: Rodopi, 1993. Ed. Raoul Granqvixt. Amsterdam: Rodopi, 1993. 151-75.

This essay examines Philip's appropriation of the English language to express the polydialectical status of African Caribbean people living in Canada (specifically), as well as elsewhere in the Caribbean Diaspora.

460.   Gowda, H. H. Anniah. "Creation in the Poetic Development of Kamau Brathwaite." *World Literature Today* 68.4 (Autumn 1994): 691-696.

Gowda examines Brathwaite's development as a poet with specific attention to the development of Brathwaite's nation language. Mini-critiques of some of Brathwaite's collections are provided in illustrating this development.

461.   Grant, Kevin, ed. *The Art of David Dabydeen.* Leeds: Peepal Tree, 1997.

This collection provides general criticism and interpretation of Dabydeen's major works. Contains interviews and bibliographic references.

462.   Guttman, Naomi. "Dream of the Mother Language: Myth and History in *She Tries Her Tongue, Her Silence Softly Breaks.*" *MELUS: The Journal of the Society for the Study of Multi-Ethnic Literature of the United States* 21.3 (Fall 1996): 53-68.

Guttman discusses four discourses from Philip's *She Tries Her Tongue, Her Silence Softly Breaks*: the aphasic, the amnesiac, the mythological, and the legal. Emphasis is placed on Philip's creation of a Caribbean myth of mother-daughter relationships created out of the discovery of the "mother-tongue."

463.   Hamner, Robert D., ed. *Critical Perspectives on Derek Walcott.* Washington, D. C.: Three Continents Press, 1993.

A comprehensive introduction to the work of Derek Walcott, this case-book contains critical essays on Walcott's writing from the 1940's into the 1970's. Ten entries are written by Walcott. These entries are accompanied by two interviews and forty critical essays. Includes a valuable 70 page annotated bibliography.

464.   _____. *Epic of the Dispossessed*. Columbia and London: University of Missouri Press, 1997.

This book length analysis of Walcott's epic poem *Omeros* is divided into eight chapters: Walcott's Odyssey, Philoctete's Wound, The Battle Over Helen, The Middle Passage – Africa, The Middle Passage - North America, The Middle Passage – Europe, The Healing, and Home From Sea.

465.   Harris, Judith. "Giotto's Invisible Sheep: Lacanian Mirroring and Modeling in Walcott's *Another Life*. *The South Atlantic Quarterly* 96 (Spring 97): 293-309.

This essay is part of a special issue on Walcott. Harris contends that Walcott positively interprets the history of the Caribbean through his synthesis of Caribbean language and lifestyles with those of Euro-America.

466.   Hornung, Alfred and Ernstpeter Ruhe, eds.   *Postcolonialism & Autobiography: Michelle Cliff, David Dabydeen, and Opal Palmer Adisa*. Amsterdam: Rodopi, 1998.

The works in this text are revised manuscripts of the above authors presented at the Anglophone workshops at the symposium on "Postcolonialism & Autobiography" which took place at Wurzburg on June 19-22, 1996.

467.   Howard, Jim. "Shaping A New Voice: The Poetry of Wilson Harris." *Commonwealth Newsl. (Aarhus)* 9 (1976): 26-31.

This discussion revolves around an analysis of selected poems from Harris' collection of poetry entitled *Fetish* (written under the pen name of Kona Waruk). Howard contends that Harris considers this collection representative of his "authentic American voice".

468.   Hoppe, John K. "From Jameson to Syncretism: The Communal Imagination of American Identity in Edward Brathwaite's *The Arrivants*. *Weber Studies* 9.3 (1992): 92-105.

This essay critiques Edward Kamau Brathwaite's *The Arrivants* against two theoretical approaches to third world literature: 1) Frederic Jameson's hermeneutic conception of cultures and 2) Wilson Harris's theories regarding cultural syncretism.

469.   Ismond, Patricia. "Another Life: Autobiography as Alternative History." *Journal of West Indian Literature* 4.1 (1990): 41-49.

Ismond contends that Walcott explores his early life as an artist in St. Lucia in an effort to work through his concern with West Indian history as negation and his overall concern with the condition of historylessness.

470.   _____. "Walcott versus Brathwaite." *Critical Perspectives on Derek Walcott.* Ed. Robert D. Hamner. Washington, DC: Three Continents, 1993. 220-36.

Ismond's comparative analysis examines Walcott's poetic insistence on the intrinsic stature of the Black that seeks to dispel notions of inferiority versus Brathwaite's poetry which embodies an elegiac mood. While there is some negativity connected with Brathwaite's approach, Ismond contends there is value in his rhythm-awareness approach.

471.   James, Cynthia. "The Unknown Text." *World Literature Today* 68.4 (Autumn 1994): 758-64.

James discusses several of Brathwaite's major works but places emphasis on several of his more obscure prose pieces and addresses. She suggests the need to compile these works into a collection in terms of positing a Caribbean aesthetic.

472.   James, Louis. "Brathwaite and Jazz." *The Art of Kamau Brathwaite.* Ed. Stewart Brown. Seren, 1995. 62-74

James discusses how Brathwaite's poetry focuses on four aspects of jazz: 1) jazz is at once folk and modern 2) jazz is not content so much as style 3) jazz is dependent on performance, and 4) jazz is continually creative.

473.   Jones, Bridget. "The Unity is Submarine: Aspects of a Pan-Caribbean Consciousness in the Work of Kamau Brathwaite." *The Art of Kamau Brathwaite.* Ed. Stewart Brown. Seren, 1995. 86-100.

This essay focuses on the elements of Brathwaite's pan-Caribbean consciousness. Emphasis is placed on the relationship of his style to Aime Cesaire.

474.   Kessler, Joyce.   "All the Horned Island's Birds: The Transformative African Symbols of Walcott's Omeros." *Arkansas Review* 5.1-2 (Aug. 1996): 1-9.

Walcott's obvious use of Western mythology is discussed alongside his not so obvious employment of African religious and literary sources to inform Achille's experiences during his journey. The use of trees, rivers, leaves, and birds as symbols is given specific attention.

475.   Kuwabong, Dannabang. "The Mother As Archetype of Self: A Poetics of Matrilineage in the Poetry of Claire Harris and Lorna Goodison." *Ariel* 30.1 (Jan. 1999): 105-29.

In this essay, Kuwabong examines the positive presentation of the mother-daughter relationship by Harris and Goodison in their writing. The essay suggests that the positive depiction of younger women (the daughter) suggests a possible reparation of historically negative depictions of women of color.

476.   Lane, M. Travis. "At Home in Homelessness: The Poetry of Derek Walcott." *Dalhousie Review* 53 (1973): 325-38.

Lane provides a close analysis of Walcott's collection of poetry, *The Gulf*. The central theme of this view is seen as the gulfs/divisions that all men live by – a type of homelessness which enables mankind to find home. Lane provides explications of several poems in *The Gulf* in support of his thesis.

477.   Livingston, James T.   "Derek Walcott's *Omeros*:   Recovering the Mythical." *Journal of Caribbean Studies* 8.3 (1991-1992): 131-40.

Livingston discusses how Walcott's epic poem *Omeros* reconnects with the ethos of Africa and the New World.   As a foundation for this discussion, he uses three ideas of Mircea Eliade (distinguished historian of religion) about myth: 1) concern with not a male or female condition, but a human condition 2) the source of all problems is the anxiety of "living in time," and 3) through employment of the mythical humans give universal expression to the basic conditions of life.

478.   Mackey, Nathaniel. "Wringing the Word." *The Art of Kamau Brathwaite*. Ed. Stewart Brown. Seren, 1995. 132-51.

In this essay Mackey analyzes Brathwaite's liberty with language in his collections *Islands, Mother Poem,* and *Sun Poem*. The discussion focuses on how Brathwaite's use of "nation language" evolves from that in the trilogy *The Arrivants* to that in the trilogy of *Mother Poem, Sun Poem, and X/Self.*

479. Maes-Jelinek, Hena, ed. *Explorations: Wilson Harris*. Dangaroo Press, 1981.

This selection of lectures and articles represents a wide range of Wilson Harris's theoretical positions from the 1960's to the 1980's. Notable selections include "The Phenomenal Legacy," "The Place of the Poet in Modern Society: A Glance at Two Guyanese Poets," and "A Talk on the Subjective Imagination."

480. Marriott, David. "Figures of Silence and Orality in the Poetry of M. Nourbese Philip." *Framing the Word: Gender and Genre in Caribbean Women's Writing.* Ed. Joan Anim-Addo. London: Whiting and Birch, 1996. 72-86.

Marriott undertakes an analysis of Philip's poetry toward understanding the debate over the status of orality and gender in Caribbean poetry and culture. Concurrently, issues of orality and black feminine discourse in terms of voice, identity, and mother tongue are explored.

481. McClure, Charlotte S. "Helen of the 'West Indies': History or Poetry Of A Caribbean Realm." *Studies in the Literary Imagination* 26.2 (Fall 1993): 7-20.

McClure presents a discussion of Walcott's ability to synthesis the old and new world, art and history, colonizer and colonized in the creation of his epic *Omeros*.

482. McCorkle, James. "Remapping the New World: The Recent Poetry of Derek Walcott." *ARIEL: A Review of International English* 17.2 (1986): 3-14.

McCorkle equates Walcott's work of this time period to "mapping" which he defines as Walcott's means of expressing the themes of self-inspection and self-definition through the use of the language of travel and exile.

483. Mikics, David. "Derek Walcott and Alejo Carpentier: Nature, History, and the Caribbean Writer." *Magical Realism: Theory, History, Community.* Eds. Lois Parkinson Zamora and Wendy B. Faris. Durham, NC: Duke University Press, 1995. 371–404.

In this essay, Mikics examines the ways in which Walcott and [other] magical realists writers, specifically Carpentier, are similar in their writing techniques. He argues that Walcott's brand of magical realism constitutes a much larger strategy of cultural mixing that is central to New World Writing.

484.   Mordecai, Pamela. "The Image of the Pebble in Brathwaite's *Arrivants.*" *Carib* 5 (1989): 60-78.

This essay examines Brathwaite's sustained use of the image of the stone, the pebble, in The Arrivants. Mordecai contends that Brathwaite masterfully extracts multiple meanings, in varying contexts, from one image.

485.   Morris, Mervyn. "Louise Bennett in Print." *Caribbean Quarterly* 28: 1-2 (1982): 44-56.

Morris discusses the value and structure of Bennett's poetry as part of both the oral and literary tradition. He presents his analysis by arguing two points: 1) that Miss Bennett's literary reputation is not well served by *Jamaica Labrish* and 2) that Miss Bennett needs to have her work conveniently available in print to assess the differences in the oral and print versions.

486.   _____. "On Reading Louise Bennett Seriously." *The Routledge Reader in Caribbean Literature*. Eds. Alison Donnell and Sarah Lawson Welsh. London and New York: Routledge, 1996. 194-197.

This essay was written by Morris in 1967 and is excerpted in this reader of Caribbean Literature. Morris makes a case for Bennett's work to be read as serious poetry by the Jamaican middle-class. He contends that Bennett's most central difficulty is choice of subject – topical issues and those of lasting interest.

487.   _____. "Overlapping Journeys: *The Arrivants.*" *The Art of Kamau Brathwaite*. Ed. Stewart Brown. Seren, 1995. 117-131.

This essay provides an introductory critical analysis of *The Arrivants*. The organization of the trilogy is discussed with an emphasis on origin, form, and technique.

488.   _____, ed. "Special Issue on Claude McKay." *Caribbean Quarterly* 38.1 (March 1992). 80 pages.

This issue was compiled to commemorate the centenary of Claude McKay's birth. The issue begins with new approaches to the studies of McKay's work with Wayne F. Cooper heading the list of contributors.

489. _____. "Walcott and the Audience for Poetry." *Critical Perspectives on Derek Walcott.* Ed. Robert D. Hamner. Washington, DC: Three Continents, 1993. 174-92.

This is the text of a lecture delivered at the Creative Arts Center at the University of the West Indies (Mona Campus) in Jamaica on March 18, 1968. Morris discusses the [then] current audience for West Indian poetry, emphasizing the work of Walcott, with suggestions for broadening that audience.

490. Parry, Benita. "Between Creole and Cambridge English: The Poetry of David Dabydeen." *Kunapipi* 10.3 (1988): 1-14.

Parry discusses Dabydeen's writing as both critic and poet. The focus here is on the use of Creole and "standard" English in his collections *Slave Song* and *Coolie Odyssey*.

491. Pollard, Velma. "An Introduction to the Poetry and Fiction of Olive Senior." *Callaloo* 11.3 (1988): 540-5.

In this essay, Pollard explores the more commonly found themes in Olive Senior's poetry and prose. She considers Senior's treatment and synthesis of issues of childhood (rural experiences) and adulthood (urban experiences) in her writing – poetry and fiction.

492. _____. "Language in the Poetry of Edward Brathwaite." *World Literature Written in English* 19 (1980): 62-74.

A look at Brathwaite's combination of theme and language is explored in this essay. *The Arrivants* is analyzed in illustrating this relationship between theme and language.

493. _____. "Overlapping Systems: Language in the Poetry of Lorna Goodison." *Carib* 5 (1989): 33-47.

This discussion of Goodison's early writing focuses on her use of English, Creole, and Dread Talk in her poetry. Pollard emphasizes Goodison's ease in moving from one code to another with a culmination of plural meaning.

494.   Povey, John. "The Search for Identity in Edward Brathwaite's *The Arrivants.*" *World Literature Written in English* 27.2 (1987): 275-289.

Povey explores content rather than form in his analysis of *The Arrivants*. He suggests that Brathwaite's personal journey described in *The Arrivants* may generate the foundation on which the principles of Caribbean aesthetics are formulated.

495.   Ramsaran, J.A. "Derek Walcott: New World Mediterranean Poet." *World Literature Written in English* 21.1 (Spring 1982): 133-147.

Ramsaran explores the ways in which Walcott's poetry synthesizes the New World Mediterranean cultures with the Old World cultures – the Mediterranean, African, and Asian.

496.   Renk, Kathleen J. "Her Words Are Like Fire: The Storytelling Magic of Dionne Brand." *Ariel* 27 (Oct. 96): 97-111.

Renk examines Brand's writing, which she contends speaks to all women and all postcolonial peoples. In doing so, she suggests that Brand's writing possesses "magic" (hope) for all those that suffer from the oppression that yet exists for postcolonial countries and their people.

497.   Rigby, Graeme. "Publishing Brathwaite: Adventures in the Video Style." *World Literature Today* 68.4 (Autumn 1994): 708-714.

A discussion of Brathwaite's "video-style" or word-sculptures on the page is presented in sections: Word-Sculpture/Word-Song, Columbus 501, Brathwaite's Dream/The Typesetter's Nightmare, and The Death of A Publication.

498.   Rohlehr, Gordon. "Dream Journeys." *World Literature Today* 68.4 (Autumn 1994): 765-74.

This essay is an abridged and revised version of the introduction to Brathwaite's *DreamStories*. The essay is divided into four sections: The Time of Salt, The Dark Village of the Dead: 4th Traveller, Sea/Sun of Misadventure: Salvages, and Unfixing the Word: Notes on Style.

499.   _____. *Pathfinder: Black Awakening in The Arrivants of Edward Kamau Brathwaite.* Port of Spain, Trinidad, 1981.

This text is considered by many literary critics to be the major critical commentary (to date) on Brathwaite's trilogy, *The Arrivants*. Rohlehr looks back at Brathwaite's literary time-line in the crafting of the trilogy. This is a very in-depth historical and biographical critique.

500. Ross, Robert L. *International Literature in English: Essays on the Major Writers*. New York: Garland Publishing, 1991.

Essays on the artistry of Caribbean writers George Lamming, Earl Lovelace, Wilson Harris, Jean Rhys, and Derek Walcott are included in this text.

501. Sander, Reinhard. "Wilson Harris's Contributions to *Kyk-over-al*: 1945-1961." *Commonwealth Literature and the Modern World*. Ed., Hena Maes-Jelinek. Brussels: Revue Des Langues Vivantes, 1975. 175-176.

This is a chronological list of Wilson's Harris's contributions to Kyk-over-al (edited by A.J. Seymour) from 1945-1961. Sander asserts that this journal is one of the most important literary magazines for the student of Caribbean literature.

502. Savory, Elaine. "En/Gendering Spaces: The Poetry of Marlene Nourbese Philip and Pamela Mordecai." *Framing the Word: Gender and Genre in Caribbean Women's Writing*. Ed. Joan Anim-Addo. London: Whiting and Birch, 1996.

Through an analysis of select poetry by Philip and Mordecai, Savory examines how complexity in their writing signals their use or manifestation of space in presenting women's [unique] ways of seeing and speaking.

503. _____. "Returning to Sycorax/Prospero's Response: Kamau Brathwaite's Word Journey." *The Art of Kamau Brathwaite*. Ed. Stewart Brown. Seren, 1995. 208-30.

Savory provides a discussion of Brathwaite's unique use of the word and the effects this usage has had on his publication history. The discussion is divided into the following categories: The Book and the Market, Returning to Sycorax: the word journey, Nommo, Nation Language, Coming Home, and Prospero's Response.

504. _____. "The Word Becomes Nam: Self and Community in the Poetry of Kamau Brathwaite, and Its Relation to Caribbean Culture and Postmodern Theory." *Writing the Nation: Self and Country in the Post-Colonial Imagination*. Ed. John C. Hawley. Amsterdam: Rodopi, 1996. 23-43.

This essay examines Brathwaite's use of "I" and "i" as denominators of self in his poetry. Savory employs Brathwaite's use of the term "nam" (soul, secret name, soul-source, connected with "nyam," eat) in examining issues of self in concert with issues of the community.

505.   Scanlon, Mara. "The Divine Body in Grace Nichol's *The Fat Black Woman's Poems*." *World Literature Today* 72.1 (Winter 1998): 59-66.

This discussion of Nichol's use of mythopoesis focuses on the first section of *The Fat Black Woman's Poems*. Scanlon examines the serious depiction of image in Nichol's seemingly playful presentation.

506.   Smilowitz, Erika. "Una Marson: Woman Before Her Time." *Jamaica Journal* 16.2 (May 1983). 62-68.

This essay is a brief documentation of Marson's life as a Jamaican poet and dramatist. Information on her role with the BBC programme "Calling the West Indies" is also discussed.

507.   _____. "Weary of Life and All My Heart's Dull Pain: The Poetry of Una Marson." *Critical Issues in West Indian Literature*. Eds. Erika Sollish Knowles and Roberta Quarles Knowles. Parkersburg, IA: Caribbean Books, 1984. 19-32.

This is a paper presented at one of the West Indian Literature Conferences held from 1981-1983. Smilowitz examines Marson as a poet who dealt primarily with issues relating to women. Her international experiences and social contributions are highlighted.

508.   Smith, Ian. "Language and Symbol in the Poetry of Dennis Scott." *Carib* (1979): 27-38.

Scott's collection *Uncle Time* is analyzed with an emphasis on his use of syntax and lineation. A discussion of symbols in Scott's poetry as elemental – sun, bird, tree, house – completes the essay.

509.   Thomas, H. Nigel. "Caliban's Voice: Marlene Nourbese Philip's Response to Western Hegemonic Discourse." *Studies in the Literary Imagination* XXVI.2 (Fall) 1993: 63-76.

Thomas addresses Philip's reconstruction of the English language [in her poetry]. Through her reconstruction, Philip deconstructs the mythology of occidental superiority, particularly through the use of language. Two key poems – "Discourse on the Logic of Language" and "Universal Grammar" - in her collection of poems *She Tries Her Tongue: Her Silence Softly Breaks* are used for this analysis.

510. Tillery, Tyrone. *Claude McKay: A Black Poet's Struggle for Identity.* Amherst, Massachusetts: University of Massachusetts Press, 1992.

This text presents a psychological view of McKay's life. Tillery studies the effect that problems of identity, vocation, and politics had on McKay and other black artists during the interwar years.

511. Torres, Saillant Silvio. "The Trials of Authenticity in Kamau Brathwaite." *World Literature Today* 68.4 (Autumn 1994): 697-707.

Silvio "defends" Brathwaite's merit as a major world poet through a discussion of his techniques in his work from 1994 backward (with the exception of the trilogies *The Arrivants* and [*Mother Poem, Sun Poem,* and *X/Self]*). The essay is organized into the following sections: Market and Alterity, Calibanism and Form, Transgressing Turfs: Disciplines and Genres, Caribbean Ways of Knowing, and The Alter Native's Authenticity.

512 Walmsley, Anne. "A Sense of Community: Kamau Brathwaite and the Caribbean Artists Movement." *The Art of Kamau Brathwaite.* Ed. Stewart Brown. Seren, 1995. 101-16.

Walmsley provides a brief history of Brathwaite's work (as co-founder) with the Caribbean Artists Movement (CAM). Emphasis is given to Brathwaite's concern with community as a concept which he acquired during his experience in Ghana.

513. Warner-Lewis, Maureen. "Africa: Submerged Mother." *The Art of Kamau Brathwaite.* Ed. Stewart Brown. Seren, 1995. 52-61.

This essay provides background on the various ways that Brathwaite seeks to integrate Africa into Caribbean history, culture, and scholarship through his poetry.

514. _____. *E. Kamau Brathwaite's "Masks": Essays and Annotations.* Rev. ed. Mona, Jamaica: Institute of Caribbean Studies, University of the West Indies, 1992.

First edition in 1977 bears the title *Notes* to "Masks." Warner-Lewis provides critical insight on *Masks,* the second part of Brathwaite's trilogy (*The Arrivants).* The text also places the work in context through an attention to West African detail and definition.

515.   Weinstein, Norman. "Jazz in the Caribbean Air." *World Literature Today*
        68.4 (1994): 715-18.

Weinstein discusses the impact that Brathwaite's early love for jazz has
had on his work as a mature poet. The discussion is organized with an
emphasis on how Brathwaite references the musicians Sonny Rollins,
John Coltrane, Albert Ayler, and Duke Ellington in his poetry.

516.   Williams, Emily Allen. *Poetic Negotiation of Identity in the Works of
        Brathwaite, Harris, Senior, and Dabydeen: Tropical Paradise Lost and
        Regained.* New York: Mellen Press, 1999.

This text is a critical examination of selected poetry by Kamau Brathwaite,
Claire Harris, Olive Senior, and David Dabydeen. The material is organized
into six chapters: Beginnings, Historical Empowerment in Edward Kamau
Brathwaite's *The Arrivants*, Claire Harris and the Poetic Shape of Women's
Words, The Ancestral Quilt of Arawak, African, and European Influence
in the Poetry of Olive Senior, David Dabydeen's Poetic Rendering of the
Centrality of Journeying in the Indo-Caribbean Experience, and Towards
the Future.

517.   _____. "Whose Words Are These"? Lost Heritage and Search for Self in
        Edward Brathwaite's Poetry." *College Language Association Journal*
        40.1 (1996): 104-11.

This essay examines the ways in which Brathwaite's poetry is bound up
in the journey, physical and metaphysical, for a sense of self and historical
identity. Williams suggests that Brathwaite's poetry moves readers
historically, socially, and psychologically through a world of dichotomized
existence toward a sense of place and self.

518.   Zackodnik, Teresa. "Writing Home: Claire Harris's *Drawing Down A
        Daughter. Ariel* 30.3 (July 1999): 163-90.

This essay examines Harris's concept of home as polyvalent and shifting
due to life's changes. Using maternal subjectivity and movement between
Trinidad and Canada, Harris presents a view of home as plurally rather
than singularly defined.

B.   Aesthetics and Theory

519.   Allis, Jeannette B. "A Case for Regional Criticism of West Indian Literature." *Caribbean Quarterly* 28: 1-2 (1982): 1-11.

In this essay Allis presents two questions – whether the critic has a responsibility as the arbiter of his society, or whether he should restrict his role to the analysis of its literature – as the basis for a need for regional [West Indian] critics to more clearly delineate and assess their own literature while not excluding the non-regional critic. While most of the works discussed are novels, this essay is useful in an overall analysis of the critique of Caribbean Literature.

520.   _____. "The Decade of the Critic: West Indian Literary Criticism in the 1970's." *Progressions: West Indian Literature in the 1970's.* Eds. Edward Baugh and Mervyn Morris. Mona, Jamaica: The University of the West Indies, 1991. 29-36.

Allis creates a thought-provoking essay by positing answers to the following questions: 1) If the 1970s is indeed the decade of the critic, how have the critics responded? 2) Are they generally following the mandate of the late sixties calling for regional commitments? 3) Are they following the paths laid down by others or are they pursuing agendas of their own?

521.   Angrosino, Michael V. "Dub Poetry and West Indian Identity." *Anthropology and Literature.* Ed. Paul Benson. Urbana: University of Illinois, 1993. 73-88.

In this essay, Angrosino asserts that dub poetry is an attempt to use nation language for the expression of political and social values of non-elite West Indians. He examines the possibility of weakening that expression if the dub poetry is translated into a more standardized poetic form.

522.   Baugh, Edward, ed. *Critics on Caribbean Literature: Readings in Literary Criticism.* New York: St. Martin's Press, 1978.

Baugh collects statements from eighteen critics who discuss works and authors across genres. Notable essays for poetry scholars are "The Muse of History" (Derek Walcott), "Blues and Rebellion: Edward Brathwaite's Rights of Passage" (Gordon Rohlehr); "The Language of West Indian Poetry" (Gerald Moore); and "The Dialect Poetry of Louise Bennett" (Mervyn Morris).

523.   _____. "West Indian Poetry 1900-1970: A Study in Cultural Decolonisation." *The Routledge Reader in Caribbean Literature.* Eds. Alison Donnell and Sarah Lawson Welsh. London and New York: Routledge, 1996. 99-104.

Baugh chronicles the development of West Indian poetry from an art form that clearly imitates the colonial foundations [of the Caribbean region] to one that begins to sound notes of individuality, albeit weak, in the generation of writers known as the Pioneers.

524.   Berry, James. "West Indian British Poetry." *Poetry Review* 73.2 (1983): 5-8.

Berry examines the growth of West Indian British poetry by positing theories surrounding its uniqueness in terms of radical subjects and intensity of feeling. Poets such as Linton Kwesi Johnson, Leslie Anthony Goffe, Errol Nelson, and Jimi Rand are discussed.

525.   Brathwaite, Edward Kamau. *Contradictory Omens: Cultural Diversity and Integration in the Caribbean.* Mona, Jamaica: Savacou Publications, 1974.

This, one of Brathwaite's early theoretical pieces, is divided into three parts (which are further divided): I) Creolization, II) Cultural Diversity, and III) Integration. Brathwaite begins the text with a series of definitions to promote clarity.

526.   _____. "English in the Caribbean: Notes on Nation Language and Poetry: An Electronic Lecture." *English Literature: Opening Up the Canon.* Eds., Leslie A. Fiedler and Houston A. Baker, Jr. Baltimore, MD:

Johns Hopkins UP, 1981. 15-53.

This is one of the selected papers presented via the English Institute [at Harvard University] in 1979. In his presentation, Brathwaite examines the shape of the English language in the Caribbean through the presentation of a historical look at its evolution(s) and form(s).

527. _____. *History of the Voice: The Development of Nation Language in Anglophone Caribbean Poetry*. London: New Beacon Books, 1984.

A lecture delivered at Harvard University, Cambridge, Massachusetts, late in August 1979. This printed version of that talk contains a bibliography of works that Brathwaite used in shaping his study of the development of "nation language."

528. _____. *The Love Axe (1): Developing A Caribbean Aesthetic, 1962-1974*. Leeds: Peepal Tree Press, 1994.

In this early monograph, Brathwaite details the development/beginning of a recognizable aesthetic accompanied by a literary criticism that moves beyond mere description. The names/work of Lewis, Wynter, Maxwell, Best, and Rohlehr are central to his analysis.

529. _____. *Roots*. The University of Michigan Press, 1993.

This is a 1993 publication of essays written throughout Kamau Brathwaite's career. The essays are "Sir Galahad and the Islands," "Roots," "Jazz and the West Indian Novel," "Caribbean Critics," "Creative Literature of the British West Indies During the Period of Slavery," "Brother Mais," " The African Presence in Caribbean Literature," and "History of the Voice."

530. Breiner, Laurence A. "The Half-Life of Performance Poems." *Journal of West Indian Literature* 8.1 (1998): 20-30.

Breiner considers the long-term canonization and understanding of performance poetry. The discussion is organized into two sections: The Text Apart from Its Performers and The Poem Apart from Its Performer.

531. _____. "How To Behave On Paper: The Savacou Debate." *Journal of West Indian Literature* 6.1: 1-10.

This essay takes a look at the debate (during the 1970s) about the printed word/poetry (scribal tradition) versus the performed word/poetry (oral tradition). The approaches of Brathwaite, Roach, and Ramchand are examined.

532.   _____. *An Introduction to West Indian Poetry*. Cambridge University Press, 1998.

This text provides a general overview of the poetry of the Anglophone Caribbean with a look at the poetry's relationship to Caribbean, European, African, and American literature. Breiner's effort is to have readers look at the poems as literary works and not just as social and political pieces.

533.   _____. "Lyric and Autobiography in West Indian Literature." *Journal of West Indian Literature* 3.1 (1989): 3-15.

This essay discusses the universality of autobiography as a literary genre with an interesting focus on the "difference" in West Indian autobiography. Breiner suggests through his analysis that West Indian autobiography moves beyond the personal and self-focus to incorporate community or what he calls "autobiography of the tribe."

534.   Brown, Lloyd. *West Indian Poetry*. 2ⁿᵈ ed. London: Heinemann, 1984.

This is a very important critical analysis (with a historical emphasis) of West Indian poetry from 1760 with the final chapter focusing on West Indian poetry since 1960. Brown provides not only history but critical analysis. This text provides an early view of West Indian poetry criticism.

535.   Collier, Gordon. "The West Indian Poetry Anthology Today." *Commonwealth Newsl.* 6 (1974): 19-26.

Collier provides a detailed look at the organization and rationale (for that organization) of seven anthologies of Anglophone Caribbean Poetry from the 1950s through the early 1970's. Most of the analysis of the importance and functional usefulness of anthologies revolves around Salkey's *Breaklight*, Ramchand and Gray's *West Indian Poetry*, and Figueroa's *Caribbean Voices*.

536.   Collins, Loretta. "Rude Bwoys, Riddim, Rub-a-Dub, and Rastas: Systems of Political Dissonance in Caribbean Performative Sounds." *Sound States: Innovative Poetics and Acoustical Technologies*. Chapel Hill, NC: U of North Carolina, 1997. 169-93.

This essay addresses the following questions: How is poetry formed out of the material conditions of cultural production? How does sound perform a national identity? How does sound establish a zeitgeist, a cooperative zeal across class lines, a desire for economic and cultural "progress". These, along with other questions, are approached through an analysis of the year 1972 [in Jamaica], the year of Michael Manley's election as Prime Minister of Jamaica and the emergence of the sound repertoires of slum dwellers, Rastafarians, Rude Boys, performance poets, and a politician with a democratic-socialist platform. A CD accompanies the book and contains a variety of tracks mentioned in the essays in the [complete] book.

537. Collins, Merle. "Themes and Trends in Caribbean Writing Today." *From My Guy to Sci-Fi*. Ed. Helen Carr. London: Pandora Press, 1989. 179-190.

This essay/paper comes out of a series of talks at the Institute of Contemporary Arts (ICA) in 1988 jointly organized by the University of London Department of Extra-Mural Studies and the ICA. Collins discusses the political themes in the writing of selected Caribbean women. Writers Louise Bennett, Merle Hodge, and Zee Edgell are discussed.

538. Cooper, Carolyn. *Noises in the Blood*. Durham, NC: Duke University Press, 1995.

In this collection of essays on Jamaican popular culture, Cooper offers an insider perspective of various cultural elements and figures. Essays cover a wide range of topics: the poetry of Louise Bennett, Jean Binta Breeze, and Mikey Smith; the mystique of dancehall and reggae; and a blend of cultural, political, and social perspectives on Caribbean popular culture.

539. Dabydeen, David. *A Handbook for Teaching Caribbean Literature*. Heinemann Educational Books, 1988.

This handbook consists of twelve units of study written by various scholars and critics on various works by Naipaul, Harris, Rhys, Selvon, Lovelace, Lamming, Anthony, Mais, Hodge, Walcott, and Brathwaite. Notable for poetry scholars are Units 11 and 12, which discuss approaches to Derek Walcott's poems (Stewart Brown) and Edward Brathwaite's poems (Nana Wilson-Tagoe).

540. Dabydeen, David and Nana Wilson-Tagoe. *A Reader's Guide to West Indian and Black British Literature*. Hansib Publishing, 1997.

This is the second revised edition. The text consists of two parts: West

Indian and Black British Literature. Each section has sub-areas of inquiry such as selected themes and notions of otherness. An appendix and select bibliography completes the text.

541.   Dabydeen, David. "On Not Being Milton: Nigger Talk in England Today." *The State of the Language*. Eds. Christopher Ricks and Leonard Michaels. Berkeley: University of California, 1990. 3-14.

Dabydeen discusses how young Black British writers are using patois in a resistance to white domination. The essay presents examples of this "radical" language in contrast to the "Queen's English."

542.   Dash, Michael. *The Other America: Caribbean Literature in a New World Context.* Charlottesville: University Press of Virginia, 1998.

Dash presents a discussion of Caribbean Literature from a Pan-Caribbean ethos and aesthetic. He synthesizes the relationship among individual imagination, national communities, regional destiny, and global history toward an understanding of new identities.

543.   D'Costa, Jean. "Oral Literature, Formal Literature: The Formation of Genre in Eighteenth Century Jamaica." *Eighteenth – Century Studies* 27.4 (1994): 663-76.

D'Costa discusses the uniqueness in the genres of Caribbean art and literature based on the racial and cultural tensions existant in the founding of Caribbean societies in the 17th and 18th centuries. The author contends that this uniqueness is most evident in the genre of drama.

544.   Fumagalli, Maria Cristina. "The Reversible World: Poetry and the West Indies." *Caribana* 5 (1996): 159-71.

In this review style essay, Fumagalli provides an analytical outline of J. Edward Chamberlin's exploratory text, *Come Back to Me My Language: Poetry and the West Indies*. Fumagalli contends that this text is a genuinely different kind of book beause of its focus on poetry and the language of West Indian poetry.

545.   Habekost, Christian. *Verbal Riddim: The Politics and Aesthetics of African-Caribbean Dub Poetry*. Atlanta, GA: Rodopi, 1993.

This text is a revised version of a doctoral dissertation accepted by the University of Mannheim (Germany) in 1991. The text is divided into two parts: I. Background (History and Development of Dub Poetry; The Sources of Word, Sound, and Power; and Riddim and Performance: The Audio-Visual Parameters) and II. Analysis (Changing Conditions of Dub Poetry's Political Discourse: Close Readings of Paradigmatic Poems; The Ghetto Experience; The Political Enemy; Campaign Poetry; Alternative Concepts; Political Purposes versus Entertainment; "We Turn Gutters Into Trenches:" Women's Dub Poetry; Into the 1990's: Revolutionary Visions and Revisions; and Future Perspectives: All Riots Reserved? The introduction provides tangible definitions of basic dub, defined dub, and critical dub.

546.   James, Louis. *Caribbean Literature in English*. London and New York: Longman, 1999.

This text is a series of essays that deal with the complexities of defining Caribbean literature in English. The essays provide historical, cultural, and aesthetic means of viewing the literature. The text is divided into five sections: "Distorting Mirrors: The Slave Era," "Anancy's Web: The Caribbean Archipelago," "Towards a Caribbean Aesthetic," "Groundation," and "On The Frontiers of Language."

547.   _____. "Caribbean Poetry in English: Some Problems." *Savacou: A Journal of the Caribbean Artists Movement* 2 (1970): 78-86.

This brief analysis considers the "problems" facing the Caribbean poet in terms of voice, attitudes, and objects or environment. The poems of Walcott, Brathwaite, Carter, and Harris are used to illustrate the terms.

548.   Jeyifo, Biodun. "On Eurocentric Critical Theory: Some Paradigms From The Texts And Sub-Texts of Post-Colonial Writing." *Critical Perspectives on Derek Walcott*. Ed. Robert D. Hamner. Washington, D.C.: Three Continents Press, 1997.

Through an analysis of Walcott's *Dream on Monkey Mountain* and *Pantomime* as paradigmatic deconstructions of Eurocentric discourse and counter-discourse, Jeyifo contends that they offer sub-texts for critical theory's engagement of Eurocentrism. Other texts such as Achebe's *Arrow of God* and Coetzee's *Waiting for the Barbarians* are suggested for further analysis of these two types of Eurocentric Critical Theory.

549.   Juneja, Renu. *Caribbean Transactions: West Indian Culture in Literature*. London: Macmillan Caribbean, 1996.

Juneja examines why West Indian writers are located in the vanguard of postcolonial literature. She contends that they have been denied the social, cultural, and political advantages other Third World writers have whose cultures have not been totally obliterated. The text is divided into eight chapters: Becoming a People, Intersecting Culture and Gender: Fiction by West Indian Women, The Backward Glance, Signifying Culture, Uses of History, V.S. Naipaul: Finding A Voice, V.S. Naipaul: Giving A Voice, and This Hybrid, This West Indian: Walcott's Epic of the New World.

550.   Killam, G. D. "Commonwealth Literary Criticism: Past, Present, and Future Prospects." *The Commonwealth Review* 1.1 (1989): 50-59.

Killiam contends that the best criticism of Commonwealth Literature will be collaborative criticism. He further asserts that the criticism should be more dynamic than static in moving from local to national and from national to local modes of critical inquiry.

551.   King, Bruce, ed. *West Indian Literature*. England: MacMillan Press, 1979.

This is an early casebook of commentary on West Indian literature (poetry and fiction) by thirteen critics. An introduction by Bruce King serves as a brief but revealing explication of early West Indian literature to the 1970s.

552.   La Fortune, K. S. "Folk Poetry in West Indian Literature." *Bim* 64 (1978): 258-68.

La Fortune contends that modern West Indian literature has its foundations in the art forms that come out of slavery and indentured labor. Select examples of folk expressions are presented throughout the essay.

553.   Marsh-Lockett, Carol P. "Centering the Caribbean Literary Imagination." *Studies in the Literary Imagination* XXVI.2 (Fall) 1993: 1-6.

As editor of the issue of *Studies in the Literary Imagination* entitled "Decolonising Caribbean Literature," this is Marsh-Lockett's editorial comment. In her opening comment, she discusses the shape of Caribbean literature – a blend of colonial and post-colonial influences. In that blending, she contends that the literature is consistently moving from margin to center.

554.   Morris, Mervyn. *Is English We Speaking and Other Essays*. Kingston, Jamaica: Ian Randle Publishers, 1999.

This text is a collection of twenty-two essays written over the years by literary critic and poet Mervyn Morris. The first nine essays focus on oral and scribal modes, performance and print, and Standard English and Creole. The introductory essay, "Is English We Speaking: West Indian Literature" captures the central focus of the entire text. Other essays of interest focus on the works of McKay, Reid, Selvon, Brathwaite, Rhys, and Walcott.

555.   _____. "A Note on 'Dub Poetry'." *Wasafiri: Journal of Caribbean, African, Asian, and Associated Literatures and Film* 26 (1997): 66-69.

In a succinctly presented discussion, Morris provides definitions of "dub poetry" and discusses the controversy surrounding the label "dub poet". Some poets recognized in this category (Oku Onuora, Linton Johnson, Mutabaruka, Jean "Binta" Breeze, Mikey Smith, and Benjamin Zephaniah) are referenced in this definition-style analysis.

556.   Nelson, Emmanuel S.   "Black America and the Anglophone Afro-Caribbean Literary Consciousness." *Journal of American Culture* 12.4 (1989): 53-58.

This comparative essay provides a brief discussion of the influence of the (revolutionary) literature and culture of Black America on the works of three Anglophone Afro-Caribbean writers: Paule Marshall, Derek Walcott, and Edward Brathwaite.

557.   Pallister, Janis L. "Outside the Monastery Walls: American Culture in Black African and Caribbean Poetry." *Journal of Popular Culture* 17.1 (1983): 74-82.

This essay examines the portrayal of American Blacks and whites in the poetry of Black African and Caribbean poets. Emphasis is placed on examples from the works of Tenreiro, Guillen, Depestre, Diallo, and Tirolien.

558.   Pearn, Julie. *Poetry in the Caribbean.* London: Hodder and Stoughton, 1985.

This text, primarily for classroom use, is an introduction to Caribbean poetry. Included is a description of its historical base and its development. Exercises appear at the end of each chapter. An introduction is written by poet Louise Bennett.

559.   Pollard, Velma. *Dread Talk: The Language of the Rastafari.* Kingston: Canoe Press, 1994.

This text is a further development of the essay "The Social History of Dread Talk." The book is a collection of papers on the speech code of the Rastafari as an example of lexical expansion.

560.   _____. "The Social History of Dread Talk." *Studies in Caribbean Language*.   Ed.   Lawrence D.   Carrington.   Trinidad: Society for Caribbean Linguistics, 1983.

This study brings respectability and linguistic recognition to the Rastafarian language which Pollard calls "Dread Talk." She explores the extension of this language into "high-brow" Jamaican society. Pollard also explores the social, historical, and philosophical contextualization processes.

561.   Putte-de Windt, Igma van. "Caribbean Poetry in Papiamentu." *Callaloo* 21.3 (1998): 654-59.

This essay provides a chronological look at the use of the Creole language Papiamentu in the islands of Aruba, Bonaire, and Curaco (part of the kingdom of the Netherlands). The essay is divided into sections: The First Milestone, The Second Milestone, The Third Milestone, and Conclusion.

562.   Ramchand, Kenneth. "Concern for Criticism." *Literary Half-Yearly* 11.2 (1970): 151-61.

In this essay Ramchand criticizes much of what was currently considered criticism during the period of his essay (the 1960s and 1970s). He contends that much of the criticism is marginal at best due to second-hand and superficial analyses of Caribbean society. Ramchand cites the critical strategies of F.R. Leavis as a start toward reparation.

563.   _____. "The Fate of Writing." *Caribbean Quarterly 28*: 1-2 (1982): 76-84.

This essay was originally presented as a paper at the Seventh Annual Conference of the Caribbean Studies Association in Kingston, Jamaica in May 1982. Ramchand attempts to illustrate the ways in which oral literature and written literature both have direct access to speech and folk elements.

564.   _____. *An Introduction to the Study of West Indian Literature*. London: Thomas Nelson and Sons, Ltd., 1976.

The chapters in this book emanate from a series of lectures given by Ramchand in the course of teaching West Indian Literature [since 1969] at the University of the West Indies [Mona Campus]. Poetry scholars will be particularly interested in Chapters 8 and 9 on Derek Walcott and [Edward] Kamau Brathwaite.

565.   _____. "Parades, Parades: Modern West Indian Poetry." *Sewanee Review* 87 (1979): 96-118.

Ramchand provides a brief historical view of West Indian poetry before discussing the major poetic voices in the West Indian poetry canon. Discussions of the works of Brathwaite, Walcott, Carter, Brown, and McNeill are included.

566.   Rodriguez, Emilio Jorge. "Oral Tradition and Recent Caribbean Poetry." *Matatu: Journal for African Culture and Society* 12 (1994): 1-12.

This essay considers *oraliture* (extra-textual presentations which cannot always be identified as literary folklore). Specifically, Rodriguez contends that some writers of recent poetry of the Anglophone Caribbean region intend the text to be a product of secondary status with the (oral) performance of the work the primary purpose.

567.   Rohlehr, Gordon. *Calypso & Society in Pre-Independence Trinidad.* Port of Spain, Trinidad, 1990.

This text examines the evolution of Trinidadian Calypso from the pre-independence period in Trinidad to the 1950s. This is a useful reference tool in that it highlights major calypsonians and those issues which have an impact on their musical (poetic) form.

568.   _____. *My Strangled City and Other Essays.* Port of Spain: Longman Trinidad Limited, 1992.

This collection of essays was written between 1970 and 1990 – a period described by Rohlehr as turbulent in Jamaica, Guyana, and Trinidad. The essays capture the essence of Caribbean life in the village and the city as well as the range of emotions involved in a journey between these locations. The essays contain direct references to the political, social, and economic changes during this period.

569.   _____. *The Shape of That Hurt and Other Essays.* Port of Spain: Longman Trinidad Limited, 1992.

This is a selection of Rohlehr's major essays written from 1980-1990. The central essay, "The Shape of That Hurt," should be read in reference to the anthology *Voiceprint*, a collection of oral and oral-related poems. The text consists of eleven essays including critiques of the works of Lamming, Carter, and Brathwaite.

570.   Sebba, Mark. "How Do You Spell Patwa?" *Critical Quarterly* 38.4 (1996): 50-63.

This essay discusses the "new" language that has developed in Britain known variously as Patois, Black English, Creole, Nation Language, or dialect. The essay is divided into sections: Creole languages, spoken and written; Creole as a written language; How do you spell Patwa?; Does Spelling Matter; The Future; and Conclusion.

571.   _____. *London Jamaican: Language Systems in Interaction.* London: Longman Press, 1993.

This socio-linguistic study examines the language use of Caribbeans [of African descent] in London. Emphasis is placed on the language of young people of the first and second British-born generations.

572.   Seymour, Arthur J. *Studies of Ten Guyanese Poems.* Georgetown: Ministry of Education, Social Development and Culture, 1982.

This text is based on a series of lectures prepared by Seymour for the students at the Lillian Dewar College of Education in 1978. Notable selections include "The Oral Tradition," "The Written Tradition," "Introduction to the Poem," and "Introduction to the Novel."

573.   _____. *West Indian Poetry: Five Essays.* Georgetown, Guyana, 1981.

This monograph grew out of a series of lectures [on teaching CXC West Indian Poetry] given by Seymour to groups in Barbados and Antigua. An introduction gives a brief overview of the history of West Indian poetry. The remaining four chapters are mini-critical analyses of the poetry of George Campbell, E. M. Roach, Philip Sherlock, and H. A. Vaughan.

574.   Torres-Saillant, Silvio. *Caribbean Poetics: Toward an Aesthetic of West Indian Literature.* New York: Cambridge University Press, 1997.

This text seeks to identify the aesthetic and cultural autonomy of Caribbean literature through the study of three Antillean authors from three different linguistic areas: Kamau Brathwaite (Barbados), Rene Depestre (Haiti), and Pedro Mir (Dominician Republic). Torres-Saillant places Caribbean poetics in the larger context of comparative poetics with a discussion of socio-political forces that interact with literary systems.

575.   Walcott, Derek. *The Antilles: Fragments of Epic Memory (The Nobel Lecture)*. New York: Farrar, Straus and Giroux, 1993.

In his Nobel Lecture, Walcott discusses the process of writing poetry with an emphasis on captured and indentured tribes creating language(s) from old, epic vocabularies.

576.   _____. "Necessity of Negritude." *Critical Perspectives on Derek Walcott*. Ed. Robert D. Hamner. Washington, D. C.: Three Continents, 1993. 20-23.

Walcott discusses the importance of Negritude in enabling poets of African descent to expand their forms of expression beyond those of a primarily European literary tradition.

577.   Warner, Keith Q. "Calypso, Reggae, and Rastafarianism: Authentic Caribbean Voices." *Popular Music and Society* 12.1 (1988): 53-62.

Warner provides a discussion of calypso, reggae, and Rastafarianism as accurate oral expressions of Caribbean political, social, and economic views. He goes further to show the unique aspects of each art form as well as the ways in which they are similar.

578.   _____. *Kaiso! The Trinidad Calypso: A Study of the Calypso as Oral Literature*. Rev. ed. Colorado: Passeggiata Press, Inc., 1999.

This book, in its third edition, is a study of the calypso as oral literature. The study is organized in six chapters: 1) The Evolution of the Calypso 2) The Language of the Calypso 3) Social and Political Commentary in the Calypso 4) Male-Female Interplay in the Calypso 5) Humor and Fantasy in the Calypso and 6) The Calypso in Trinidad Literature.

C. Gender and Sexuality

579.   Adisa, Opal Palmer. "De Language Reflect Dem Ethos: Some Issues With Nation Language." *Winds of Change: The Transforming Voices of Caribbean Women Writers and Scholars*. Eds. Adele S. Newson and Linda Strong-Leek. New York: Peter Lang, 1998. 17-31.

This paper was presented at t he 1996 International Conference of Caribbean Women Writers and Scholars held at Florida International University. Adisa discusses Caribbean women writers' efforts to use language to convey necessary meanings to their audiences as they feel necessary. The use of Creole, patois, nation language, and standard language forms is addressed.

580.   Aho, William R. "Sex Conflict in Trinidad Calypsoes 1969-1979." *Revista/ Review Interamericana* 11.1 (Spring 1981): 76-81.

This essay is an empirical analysis of male-female conflict as reflected in the lyrics of 311 calypsoes.

581.   Bloom, Harold, ed. *Caribbean Women Writers*. Philadelphia, PA: Chelsea House Publishers, 1997.

In the Frontispiece, "The Analysis of Women Writers," Bloom contends that different aesthetic standards do not apply to female and male writers. With that focus in view, Bloom compiles a number of critical extracts (from books, essays, and monographs) in analyzing the works of Caribbean women writers Phyllis Shand Alfrey, Erna Brodber, Michelle Cliff, Merle Collins, Edwidge Danticat, Zee Edgell, Beryl Gilroy, Merle Hodge, Jamaica Kincaid, Paule Marshall, Jean Rhys, and Olive Senior. Each author's section contains a short biographical statement.

582.   Chancy, Myriam J. A. *Searching for Safe Spaces: Afro-Caribbean Women Writers in Exile.* PA: Temple University Press, 1997.

This critical examination focuses on the writing of Afro-Caribbean women writers with an emphasis on their exile from their home islands. Chancy pays close attention to issues of race, sex, sexuality, class, age, and nationality as they are reflected in the writing. Writers M. Nourbese Philip, Dionne Brand, Michelle Cliff, and others are highlighted.

583.   Cobham, Rhonda. "Women in Jamaican Literature, 1900-1950." *Out of the Kumbla: Caribbean Women and Literature.* Eds. Carole Boyce Davies and Elaine Savory Fido. Trenton, New Jersey: Africa World Press, Inc., 1990. 195-222.

This essay examines the depiction of Jamaican women in the writings of Claude McKay, H.G. DeLisser, T.H. MacDermot, J.E. Clare McFarlane, Una Marson, George Campbell, Vice Reid, Louise Bennett, and others.

584.   Collins, Merle. "Orality and Writing: A Revisitation." *Winds of Change: The Transforming Voices of Caribbean Women Writers and Scholars.* Eds. Adele S. Newson and Linda Strong-Leek. New York: Peter Lang, 1998. 37-45.

This essay/paper was presented at the 1996 International Conference of Caribbean Women Writers and Scholars held April 24-27 at Florida International University. Collins discusses the ways in which orality and writing are connected. Through a series of references to specific texts and writers, Collins provides means of examining how aspects of the performance mode are incorporated in written work.

585.   Cudjoe, Selwyn R. "Choosing Exile: Black Women Writers from the Caribbean." *Defining Ourselves: Black Writers in the 90s.* Eds. Elizabeth Nunez and Brenda M. Greene. New York: Peter Lang, 1999. 75-85.

Cudjoe examines the elements that make Caribbean women writers' works so powerful and how their style is intimately tied to that of African American women writers. Issues of exile and culture as central in the writing are highlighted through references to specific texts and writers. (This was one of the papers presented at the Fourth National Black Writers Conference in 1996).

586.   Dance, Daryl Cumber. "Matriarchs, Doves, and Nymphos: Prevalent Images of Black, Indian, and White Women in Caribbean Literature." *Studies in the Literary Imagination* 26.2 (Fall 1993): 21-31.

Dance examines the often stereotypical portrayals of women - Black, Indian, and White – by male Caribbean writers. This essay represents an early look at a very controversial issue in Caribbean literature.

587.   Davies, Carol Boyce and Elaine Savory Fido, eds. *Out of the Kumbla: Caribbean Women and Literature.* New Jersey: Africa World Press, 1990.

This text provides a variety of critical and analytical essays on the literature of Caribbean women writers. The essays are organized in three sections: Woman Consciousness: Righting History and Redefining Identity in Caribbean Literature, Constricting and Expanding Spaces: Women in Caribbean Literature, and Caribbean Women Writers: Redefining Caribbean Literature. A Foreword is written by Pamela Mordecai.

588.   Ellis, Pat, ed. *Women of the Caribbean.* Jamaica: Kingston Publishers Ltd., 1985.

This text, with a comprehensive introduction by Pat Ellis, presents a variety of essays on women in the Caribbean. A notable section for poetry scholars is Part 5: Women and Culture, which includes essays by Cheryl Williams, Claudette Earl, Elma Reyes, and Honor Ford-Smith.

589.   Fenwick, M. J. "Female Calibans: Contemporary Women Poets of the Caribbean." *The Zora Neale Hurston Forum* 4.1 (1989): 1-8.

Fenwick's essay is an exploration of the literary offerings of contemporary women poets in the Caribbean whose expressions defy the traditional colonial models. Works of poets Lorna Goodison, Jean Goulbourne, Cyrene Tomlinson, Jennifer Brown, and others are used in this analysis.

590.   Ferguson, Moira. *Colonialism and Gender Relations from Mary Wollstonecraft to Jamaica Kincaid.* New York: Columbia University Press, 1993.

This text closely examines the connections between gender and colonial relations in texts by British writers of the eighteenth and nineteenth centuries and Caribbean writers of the nineteenth and twentieth centuries: Mary Wollstonecraft, Anne Hart Gilbert, Elizabeth Hart Thwaites, Jane Austen, Jean Rhys, and Jamaica Kincaid.

591.   Fido, Elaine. "Crossroads: Third World Criticism and Commitment with Reference to African-Caribbean Women Poets." *ACLALS Bulletin* 7.5 (1986): 10-25.

Fido discusses the poetry of three poets of African descent – Christine Craig, Lorna Goodison, and Esther Philips – in terms of how each writes different aspects of their experience into their poetry. She examines the relationship between their writing and the reader/critic/audience in the creative process.

592.   Gilkes, Michael. "The Madonna Pool: Women as 'Muse of Identity'." *Journal of West Indian Literature* 1.2 (1987): 1-19.

Gilkes examines a number of literary works in their employment of the image of woman as Muse. The author suggests that a movement to the androgynous figure in Caribbean literature will be more prevalent with the increase of Caribbean women writers.

593.   Hunter, Lynette. "After Modernism: Alternative Voices in the Writings of Dionne Brand, Claire Harris, and Marlene Philip." *University of Toronto Quarterly: A Canadian Journal of the Humanities* 62.2 (1992-93): 256-81.

This essay is a discussion of the issues of race, access, and verbal tradition in the writing of Dionne Brand, Claire Harris, and Marlene Philip. The three live and work in Canada and are originally from the Republic of Trinidad and Tobago.

594.   Ippolito, Emilia. *Caribbean Women Writers: Identity and Gender.* Rochester, NY: Camden House, 2000.

This text examines the prolific literary production of Caribbean writers in the 1980s and 1990s with an emphasis on the works of Jamaica Kincaid, Erna Brodber, Marlene Nourbese Philip, and Merle Hodge. Poetry scholars will be particularly interested in the analyses of works by Marlene Nourbese Philip.

595.   Ismond, Patricia. "Women as Race-Containing Symbol in Walcott's Poetry." *Journal of West Indian Literature* 8.2 (1999): 83-90.

Ismond examines the early critique of Walcott's writing as patriarchial and sexist in focus and content. She focuses on a major shift of sensibility in his work of the late 1970's in connection with the women's movement.

596.   Kuwabong, Dannabang. "The Mother As Archetype of Self: A Poetics of Matrilineage in the Poetry of Claire Harris and Lorna Goodison." *ARIEL: A Review of International English Literature* 30.1 (1999): 105-29.

This essay provides a view toward how Claire Harris and Lorna Goodison highlight and celebrate the role of the mother in their writing. Harris, Goodison, and a number of other writers in the African-Caribbean literary tradition are viewed as creating matrilineal icons.

597.   Lee, Valerie. "The Female Voice in Afro-American and Afro-Caribbean Poetry." *Umoja* 3 (1979): 175-84.

This essay focuses on changes in the poetry of women of Afro-Caribbean and Afro-American descent. Topical changes and expansions from that of men in these cultures are the female concerns with childhood, man/woman relations, and womanhood. Lee contends that Third World women have the additional burden of dealing with racial and sexual stereotypes, which emerges in their writing.

598.   Liddell, Janice and Yakini Belinda Kemp, eds. *Arms Akimbo: Africana Women in Contemporary Literature*. Florida: UP of Florida, 1999.

While this is a collection of critical essays on the fictions of Africana women writers, poetry scholars will find the essays insightful in broadly analyzing the positions and views of Africana women writers. Essays on the writing of Paule Marshall, Ama Ata Aidoo, Mariama Ba, Buchi Emecheta, Jamaica Kincaid, Sherley Anne Williams, Sylvia Wynter, and others are included.

599.   Mohammed, Patricia. "Women's Response in the 70's and 80's in Trinidad: A Country Report." *Caribbean Quarterly* 35.1-2 (March-June 1989): 36-45.

This essay appears in the issue of *Caribbean Quarterly* entitled "Women and Caribbean Development." Mohammed considers the image of women in recent calypsos by both men and women.

600.   Morrell, Carol, ed. *Grammar of Dissent: Poetry and Prose by Claire Harris, M. Nourbese Philip, Dionne Brand*. Fredericton: Goose Lane Editions, 1994.

Morrell has selectively gathered the poetry of these Trinidad and Tobago-born writers, currently living in Canada, into this text. The selected work highlights the concerns of Harris, Philip, and Brand with the state of the lives of [Caribbean] immigrants, particularly those living in Canada.

601.   Paravisini-Gebert, Lizabeth. "Women Against the Grain: The Pitfalls of Theorizing Caribbean Women's Writing." *Winds of Change: The Transforming Voices of Caribbean Women Writers and Scholars.* Eds. Adele S. Newson and Linda Strong-Leek. New York: Peter Lang, 1998. 161-68.

This paper was presented at the 1996 International Conference of Caribbean Women Writers and Sch olars held at Florida International University. In her discussion, Paravisini-Gebert contends that there is a risk to Caribbean women's writing – that of being coerced from the realities of their own specific languages, cultures, religions, and traditions of their islands by the various perspectives offered by postcolonial studies.

602.   Pollard, Velma. "Language and Identity: The Use of Different Codes in Jamaican Poetry." *Winds of Change: The Transforming Voices of Caribbean Women Writers and Scholars.* Eds. Adele S. Newson and Linda Strong-Leek. New York: Peter Lang, 1998. 31-36.

This paper was presented at the 1996 International Conference of Caribbean Women Writers and Scholars held at Florida International University. Pollard analyzes one poem by Lorna Goodison, "Ocho Rios II," to illustrate the use of different codes in Jamaican poetry. Pollard focuses on Goodison's use of three codes: Jamaican English, Jamaican Creole, and Dread Talk.

603.   Savory, Elaine. "Ex/Isle: Separation, Memory, and Desire in Caribbean Women's Writing." *Winds of Change: The Transforming Voices of Caribbean Women Writers and Scholars.* Eds. Adele S. Newson and Linda Strong-Leek. New York: Peter Lang, 1998.

This paper was presented at the 1996 International Conference of Caribbean Women Writers and Scholars held at Florida International University. In her discussion, Savory distinguishes between the term "exile" and what she calls "ex/isle" as differing based on the Caribbean woman writer's desire – the origin of writing.

604.   Thompson, Thelma B. "Their Pens, Their Sword: New Jamaican Women Poets and Political Statement in Nation Language." *Studies in the*

Literary Imagination 26 (Fall 1993): 45-62.

This essay deals with the contemporary works of female Jamaican poets which utilize "nation language" as a means of asserting pride, rejecting restrictions of traditional form and emphasizing audience inclusion rather than exclusion.

605.   Waldman, Gloria Feiman. "Affirmation and Resistance: Women Poets from the Caribbean". *Contemporary Women Authors of Latin America: Introductory Essays*. Ed. Doris Meyer. Brooklyn, NY: Brooklyn College Publishers, 1983. 33-57.

Waldman examines the poetry of Louise Bennett of Jamaica; the poetry of Lolita Lebron, Iris Landron, Elsa Tio, and Maria Arrillaga from Puerto Rico; and the poetry of Belkis Ciuza Male and Nancy Morejon from Cuba. Her examination reveals a commonality of themes, concerns, and technical styles.

D. History and Culture

606.   Abrahams, Roger D. "Child Ballads in the West Indies: Familiar Fabulations, Creole Performances." *Journal of Folklore Research* 24.2 (1987): 107-134.

Through a concentration on performances of child ballads in public arenas in the West Indies, Abrahams explores the language of the marketplace (in opposition to that of the village and homestead) in terms of a discussion on traditions and conventions of performance.

607.   _____. *Man of Words in the West Indies: Performance and the Emergence of Creole Culture.* Baltimore: Johns Hopkins Press, 1983.

In this study, Abrahams documents the social folkways and mores of the culture with significant attention to language use. This study is now considered one of the most important early works on creole culture and its history.

608.   Arnold, A. James, ed. *A History of Literature in the Caribbean.* Vol. 3. Amsterdam: John Benjamins Publishing Company, 1997.

This text is one of a series of works in the Comparative History of Literatures in European Languages sponsored by the International Comparative Literature Association. Essays by various scholars are assembled under the following headings: Preliminary Approaches, Literary Creoleness and Chaos Theory, Problematics of Literary Historiography, Literature and Popular Culture, Carnival and Carnivalization, Gender and Identity, The Caliban Complex, Genre and Postcoloniality, and Cross-Cultural Currents and Conundrums.

609.   Brannigan, John. "The Regions Caesar Never Knew: Cultural Nationalism and the Caribbean Literary Renaissance in England." *Jouvert: A Journal of Postcolonial Studies* 5.1 (2000).

This is a narrative listing of thirty-eight entries which provide details on significant events, people, and ideologies that merge in the formation of cultural nationalism and the Caribbean Literary Renaissance in England. The listing is a clear-cut means of accessing a wealth of information in short-takes.

610.   Brathwaite, Edward Kamau. "History, the Caribbean Writer and *X/Self.*" *Crisis and Creativity in the New Literatures in English.* Eds. Geoffrey V. Davis and Hena Maes-Jelinek. Rodopi, 1999.

Brathwaite discusses the importance of knowledge of the history of the Caribbean in the creation of his poetry. He contends that his poetry moved to a new level when the history of the Caribbean, albeit fragmented, began to be tangible.

611.   Brown, Stewart. "Poet in Opposition." *Index on Censorship* 9.5 (1980): 32-36.

This essay, though brief, provides a chronological view of the evolution of Carter's poetry as a display of political fervor to that of a type of political acquiescence. The essay provides a view toward the overall position of writers in the pre and post - independence Caribbean.

612.   Burnett, Paula.   "'Where Else to Row, But Backward?' Addressing Caribbean Futures through Re-visions of the Past." *ARIEL: A Review of International English Literature* 30.1 (Jan. 1999): 11-37.

Using Walcott's ideas from "The Muse of History" as a framework, Burnett discusses the use of history and myth in Caribbean Literature. She uses recent texts by V. S. Naipaul, Wilson Harris, Derek Walcott, Pauline Melville, David Dabydeen, and Fred D'Aguiar.

613.   Chamberlin, J. Edward. *Come Back To Me My Language: Poetry and the West Indies.* University of Illinois Press, 1993.

This text presents a critical look at more than thirty Caribbean poets and how their works incorporate African and British colonial traditions. The text is divided into six sections: A black apostrophe to pain, Where then is the nigger's home?, Come back to me my language, To court the language of my people, Loose now the salt cords binding our tongues, and i a tell no tale.

614.   Croxford, Agnes M. "Nature and History in the Search for a Concept of Self in the Poetry of English-Canada and the West Indies." *Black i: A Canadian Journal of Black Expression* 2.1 (1973): 33-35, 45.

This essay explores the differences in Canadian poets' and West Indian poets' use of nature and history in developing identification platforms. The essay is divided into two sections, each of which deals exclusively with the nuances in nature and history that each group accesses in their quests for identity.

615.   Dabydeen, Cyril. "Places We Come From: Voices of Caribbean Canadian Writers (in English) and Multi-Cultural Contexts." *World Literature Today* 73.2 (Spring 1999): 231-7.

This essay is part of a special issue on contemporary Canadian Literature. Dabydeen discusses the evolution and present condition of Caribbean-Canadian Literature. He provides an interesting rebuttal to the notion that multi-cultural Canadian literature is diluting Canadian Literature.

616.   Dathorne, O. R. *Dark Ancestor: The Literature of the Black Man in the Caribbean.* Louisiana State University Press, 1981.

In eight chapters, Dathorne considers the foundation(s) of Blacks (of African heritage) in the Caribbean Basin region. Contains a detailed bibliography organized by genre categories.

617.   Dexter, Noel. "Folk Song Performance in the Caribbean." *Caribbean Quarterly* 29.1 (1983): 66-69.

This essay highlights the attention which is currently being directed to the folk tradition in the Caribbean region through a brief analysis of the development in Caribbean folk songs. CARIFESTA is cited as an excellent venue for witnessing the wide range of diversity in the arrangements and performances of Caribbean folk songs.

618.   Ellis, Keith. "Images of Sugar in English and Spanish Caribbean Poetry."
           ARIEL: A Review of International English Literature 24.1 (1993): 149-59.

           Ellis discusses the use of sugar as a symbolic device in selected Caribbean
           poetry written in English and Spanish. The essay explores both the
           conscious and unconscious use of sugar in the writing.

619.   Harvey, Stefano. *Nationalism and Identity: Culture and the Imagination
           in a Caribbean Diaspora*. Atlantic Highlands, NJ: Zed Books, 1996.

           This text is a study of the forces and ideologies of nationalism on the
           literary imagination of writers from Trinidad and Tobago. Works by V. S.
           Naipaul, C. L. R. James, Willi Chen, Valerie Belgrave, Earl Lovelace,
           Michael Anthony, Samuel Selvon, and Neil Bissoondath are used in this
           analysis.

620.   Healy, Jack. "Reflections on the Kingston Commonwealth Conference
           and West Indian Literature." *ACLALS Bulletin* (1974): 32-40.

           This essay recounts some of the major issues presented and discussed at
           the third conference of ACLALS held in the West Indies. The conference,
           held at the University of the West Indies (Mona) in Jamaica, was the first
           time West Indian writers had gathered in the West Indies to discuss their
           literature.

621.   Hogan, Patrick Colm. *Colonialism and Cultural Identity: Crises of
           Tradition in the Anglophone Literatures of India, Africa, and the
           Caribbean*. Albany, NY: State University of New York, 2000.

           Hogan analyzes the issue of cultural identity by using literary works,
           primarily those written in English. He argues that the problems of colonial-
           ism and cultural identity are often contradictory and always problematic.
           An "Analytical Glossary of Selected Theoretical Concepts" provides an
           overview of the book's major theoretical concepts.

622.   Kaup, Monika. "West Indian Canadian Writing: Crossing the Border from
           Exile to Immigration." *Essays on Canadian Writing* 57 (1995): 171-93.

           Kaup presents an overview of the West Indian literary presence in Canada.
           Emphasis is placed on the work of Austin Clarke, Dionne Brand, and Neil
           Bissoondath.

623.   Lalla, Barbara and Jean D'Costa. *Language in Exile: Three Hundred
           Years of Jamaican Creole*. Tuscaloosa, Alabama: Alabama University
           Press, 1990.

This text is a documentation of the history of Jamaican Creole. Divided into two parts, Part I is a linguistic analysis of the data in Part II, which is a selection of texts from works written in and around Jamaica from the 17th through the 19th centuries.

624.   Nettleford, Rex. *Caribbean Cultural Identity: The Case of Jamaica*. Los Angeles: UCLA Center for Afro-American Studies, 1979.

This study examines Eurocentrism in Caribbean societies and how it sets up conflict in the Caribbean psyche. Nettleford looks at indigenous and foreign ideologies which lead to a schizoid, bi-cultural mindset.

625.   Pedersen, Carl. "Middle Passages: Representations of the Slave Trade in Caribbean and African-American Literature." *Massachusetts Review* (Summer 1992): 225-228.

Pedersen undertakes a reconceptualization of the Middle Passage through an analysis of five texts: Olaudah Equianao's *The Interesting Narrative of the Life of Olaudah Equiano or Gustavus Vassa, the African*, George Lamming's *Natives of My Person*, Edward Kamau Brathwaite's *The Arrivants*, Robert Hayden's *Middle Passage*, and Charles Johnson's *Middle Passage*.

626.   Poynting, Jeremy. "From Shipwreck to Odyssey: One Hundred Years of Indo-Caribbean Writing." *Wasafiri* 21 (Spring 1995): 56-57.

Poynting examines the growth and change in Indo-Caribbean writing over a hundred year period. He contends that much of the change stems from a movement away from a sense of marginality in the post 1970s period. Focus is on "bung coolie" culture writing, Indo-Caribbean women's writing, location of a tradition of Indian literary aesthetics and poetics, and writing the Indo-Caribbean experience outside of the Caribbean.

627.   Ramchand, Kenneth. "Columbus in Chains." *Wasafiri* 16 (Autumn 1992): 19-20.

This article is taken from Ramchand's 1989 Walter Rodney lecture at the University of Warwick. Ramchand considers Columbus, the historical figure, as a focal point of many themes and motifs in West Indian Literature.

628.   Ramraj, Victor J. "West Indian-Canadian Writing in English." *International Journal of Canadian Studies* 13 (1996): 163-68.

This essay presents a brief history of the West Indian literary presence in Canada from Austin Clarke to present writers such as Cyril Dabydeen, Sasenarine Persaud, Claire Harris, Dionne Brand, M. Nourbese Philip, and Lillian Allen.

629.   Saakana, Amon Saba. *The Colonial Legacy in Caribbean Literature.* New Jersey: Africa World Press, 1987.

This is a discussion of colonization and its effects on the Caribbean literary tradition. Emphasis is on a modernist look at decolonization. A prefatory note, "Decolonization" is written by Ngugi wa Thiong'o. The text is divided into seven chapters: "Socialisation & Struggle in the Nineteenth," "Towards A Beginning: Literature & Life in the Nineteenth Century," "Language & the Shaping of Consciousness," "Trauma & Bourgeois Nationalism: Buckra's Perspectives," "Nationalism & Race Consciousness? 1900-1944," "Education of a Colonial & The Lost Centre of V.S. Naipaul," and "Migration of the Spirit: The Old World."

630.   Sander, Reinhard W.   "The Impact of Literary Periodicals on the Development of West Indian Literature and Cultural Independence." Ed. Hena Maes-Jelinek. *Commonwealth Literature and the Modern World.* Brussels: Revue Des Langues Vivantes, 1975. 25-32.

This paper was delivered at a conference on Commonwealth Literature held at the University of Liege from April 2-5, 1974. In this talk, Sander discusses the contribution of the three literary magazines – *The Beacon, Bim,* and *Kyk-over-al* – to the development of West Indian literature and cultural independence. He reveals the political thrust of each magazine/ journal as well its role in introducing new writers to West Indian audiences.

631.   _____. *The Trinidad Awakening: West Indian Literature of the Nineteen Thirties.* New York: Greenwood Press, 1988.

This study of the literary activity in Trinidad during the 1930s provides broad implications for the general study of West Indian Literature. The text contains a background on Trinidad from 1919-1938, an overview of the magazines *Trinidad* and *The Beacon*; a synopsis of the short fiction of the period; chapters on Alfred Mendes, C.L.R. James, and Ralph Boissiere; and a bibliography.

632.   Thieme, John. "Pre-Text and Con-Text." *(Un)Writing Empire.* Ed. Theo D'haen. Amsterdam: Rodopi, 1998. 81-98.

This essay examines a number of Anglophone Caribbean texts in assessing whether their use of European texts as a base actually contests or supports the notion of a hegemonic authority of these texts. Works by Mighty Sparrow, Jean Rhys, Sam Selvon, Caryl Phillips, Olive Senior, Erna Brodber, and Derek Walcott are considered.

633.   Walmsley, Anne. "The Caribbean Artists Movement 1967-72: Its Inauguration and Significance (research in progress)." *Wasafiri* 5 (Autumn 1986): 3-7.

While this is a short, exploratory essay on the formation and impact of The Caribbean Artists Movement (CAM), it provides key information for further inquiry. Key people, places, and events leading up to, during, and after the formal operation of CAM are provided.

634.   _____. *The Caribbean Artists Movement 1966-1972: A Literary and Cultural History.* London & Port-of-Spain: New Beacon Books, 1992.

This text expands upon the research done in Walmsley's previous essay published in *Wasafiri* in 1986. The author was an active member of CAM from 1967 onwards and writes from an insider position.

E.   Politics and Race

635.   Bery, Ashok and Patricia Murray, eds. *Comparing Postcolonial Literatures: Dislocations.* Great Britain: Macmillan Press, 2000.

This collection of essays forms a comparative study of the historical, cultural, and political legacies of colonialism pertaining to different cultural and racial groups. The text is divided into four sections: On the Border, Diasporas, Internalized Exiles, and Versions of Hybridity.

636.   Cudjoe, Selwyn Reginald. *Resistance and Caribbean Literature.* Athens: Ohio University Press, 1980.

In this text, Cudjoe provides a major analysis of the historical background of the Caribbean toward the formation of rational ideologies and theories of Caribbean literature. Organized into nine chapters (divided into Parts I and II), Part I analyzes the history of Caribbean resistance with Part II examining specific works which embody and present modes of resistance.

637.   Edmondson, Belinda J., ed. *Caribbean Romances: The Politics of Regional Representation.* Charlottesville, VA: University of Virginia Press, 1999.

Edmondson uses "romance" to describe the idealized representations of Caribbean society. The ten essays focus on the ways the romance trope is used with Caribbean political-social-historical discourses in the discussion of "new" postcolonial societies in the Caribbean region.

638.   _____. "Race, Tradition, and the Construction of the Caribbean Aesthetic." *New Literary History* 25 (Winter 94): 109-20.

The writer examines ideological conceptions of essential blackness through an analysis of selected work of Kamau Brathwaite and C.L.R. James. Edmondson concludes that black aesthetic ideologies are not wholly problematic but some of the theories that support such ideologies.

639.   Henry, Paget and Paul Buhle, eds. *C. L. R. James's Caribbean*. Durham, NC: Duke University Press, 1992.

This text provides insight into some of James' lesser-known work and writings about the politics and culture of the Caribbean region. The editors compile essays that address James' theories on difference and similarity in the developing and more advanced areas of the Caribbean.

640.   Larrier, Renee. "Racism in the United States: An Issue in Caribbean Poetry." *Journal of Caribbean Studies* 2.1 (1981): 51-71.

While this essay focuses on the manner in which the poetry of French and Spanish speaking Caribbean poets of the twentieth century reflects the influence of the African American revolutionary spirit and unity, it nevertheless provides a broad view of the dominant themes of Caribbean poets – Anglophone, Francophone, and Hispaniophone. Larrier explores how writers are affected not only by social and political forces but also by literary movements.

641.   Needham, Anuradha Dingwaney. *Using the Master's Tools: Resistance and the Literature of the African and South-Asian Diasporas*. New York: St. Martins, 2000.

This text focuses on C.L.R. James, Salman Rushdie, Ama Ata Aidoo, Michelle Cliff, and Hanif Kureishi – writers who are from formerly colonized countries of the Caribbean, Africa, and South Asia – who incorporate resistance in their texts. Chapter 4, "Retracing the African Part of Ourselves: Identity in the Work of Michelle Cliff" will be of particular interest to Caribbean poetry scholars.

642.   Taylor, Patrick. *The Narrative of Liberation: Perspectives on Afro-Caribbean Literature, Popular Culture, and Politics*. Ithaca: Cornell University Press, 1989.

Taylor focuses on the experiences of the Afro-Caribbean community, particularly those dominated by British, French, (and later) American colonialism. Six chapters deal with Frantz Fanon, Colonialism and its Drama, Vaudou, Negritude, and The Liberation of Narrative via a view of works by George Lamming and Derek Walcott.

VI. Interviews

643.   Dance, Daryl Cumber. "Conversation with Louise Bennett." *New World Adams: Conversations with Contemporary West Indian Writers.* Leeds: Peepal Tree Press, 1992. 25-30.

This interview took place on Friday, September 15, 1978, at Louise Bennett's home in Gordon Town. The focus, largely on Jamaican folklore, provides information on her writing influences and techniques.

644.   _____. "Conversation with Jan Carew." *New World Adams: Conversations with Contemporary West Indian Writers.* Leeds: Peepal Tree Press, 1992. 31-43.

This interview took place in Chicago on November 21, 1980. At the time, Carew and his wife were teaching at universities in the area. While most of the discussion focuses on his novels and plays, readers will find the discussionn about his writing style important when reading his poetry collections, *Streets of Eternity* (1952) and *Sea Drums in My Blood (1981).*

645.   _____. "Conversation with Wilson Harris." *New World Adams: Conversations with Contemporary West Indian Writers.* Leeds: Peepal Tree Press, 1992. 79-95.

This interview was conducted in New York City on May 13, 1980. Harris discusses a critical study in progress, race and writing, and his overall approach to writing. The discussion will provide insight for readers approaching his collection of poetry *Eternity to Season* (revised in 1978).

646.   _____. "Conversation with Anthony McNeill." *New World Adams: Conversations with Contemporary West Indian Writers.* Leeds: Peepal Tree Press, 1992. 159-168.

This interview was conducted in McNeill's office at the Institute of Jamaica in Kingston on March 2, 1980. Readers who have struggled to understand his poetry [e.g., *Hello Ungod* (1971), *Reel from 'The Life Movie,'* (1972, revised 1975), and *Credences at the Altar of Cloud* (1979)] will appreciate this illuminating discussion of his philosophy and writing approach.

647.   _____. "Conversation with Pam Mordecai and Velma Pollard." *New World Adams: Conversations with Contemporary West Indian Writers.* Leeds: Peepal Tree Press, 1992. 169-181.

This dual interview was conducted in Pamela Mordecai's office at the University of the West Indies in Kingston on March 12, 1980. The two writers talk about their womanist approach to their writing while declining the title of feminist. Influences are discussed as well.

648.   _____. "Conversation with Mervyn Morris." *New World Adams: Conversations with Contemporary West Indian Writers.* Leeds: Peepal Tree Press, 1992. 183-191.

This interview took place at Morris's home on November 17, 1978. Morris discusses his family, education, writing styles, and favorite writers. Readers will find certain responses to questions about poems revealing.

649.   _____. "Conversation with Dennis Scott." *New World Adams: Conversations with Contemporary West Indian Writers.* Leeds: Peepal Tree Press, 1992. 218-227.

This interview was conducted in Jamaica on Tuesday, March 11, 1980. Scott talks about his early education and his poetry collections. He responds to Dance's questions about critical response and comments on his poetry.

650.   _____. "Conversation with Derek Walcott." *New World Adams: Conversations with Contemporary West Indian Writers.* Leeds: Peepal Tree Press, 1992. 255-264.

This interview was conducted at Dance's home in Richmond, VA on March 3, 1981. Walcott spends a great deal of the interview talking about his family background and how it affects the style and content of his writing. Issues of race and color are at the center of this interview.

651.   ____. *New World Adams: Conversations with Contemporary West Indian Writers*. Leeds: Peepal Tree Press, 1992.

This text is a collection of interviews compiled by Daryl Dance. She explores a range of issues that impact upon the writers (novelists and poets) in her examination of the West Indian literary aesthetic.

652.   Dawes, Kwame, ed. "James Berry." *Talk Yuh Talk: Interviews with Anglophone Caribbean Poets*. Charlottesville, VA: University of Virginia Press, 2001. 1-10.

Berry was born in rural Jamaica in 1924. Dawes' interview focuses on Berry's writing stemming from a unique Jamaican and British sensibility, homogenous in nature.

653.   ____. "Martin Carter." *Talk Yuh Talk: Interviews with Anglophone Caribbean Poets*. Charlottesville, VA: University of Virginia Press, 2001. 11-21.

Martin Carter, born and educated in Guyana, lived from 1927-1988. His early poetry, decidedly political, marks his legacy as a Caribbean writer. The interview in this text was conducted by Fred D'Aguiar.

654.   ____. "Kamau Brathwaite." *Talk Yuh Talk: Interviews with Anglophone Caribbean Poets*. Charlottesville, VA: University of Virginia Press, 2001. 22-37.

Brathwaite was born in Barbados in 1930. He is considered one of the two major poets in Caribbean Literature (the other being Derek Walcott). This interview reflects Brathwaite's eclectic style in not simply responding to essay questions but reaching back to the past and projecting into the future in building his responses.

655.   ____. "Edward Baugh." *Talk Yuh Talk: Interviews with Anglophone Caribbean Poets*. Charlottesville, VA: University of Virginia Press, 2001. 38-46.

Baugh was born in Jamaica in 1936. This interview focuses on his limited production as a poet and his more expansive reputation as a critic and professor of English Literature at the University of the West Indies (Mona). Dawes tries to find out the reasons for Baugh's focus in the interview.

656.   _____. "Mervyn Morris." *Talk Yuh Talk: Interviews with Anglophone Caribbean Poets.* Charlottesville, VA: University of Virginia Press, 2001. 47-60.

Morris, born in 1937, has taught at the University of the West Indies (Mona) since the mid-1960s. In this interview, Dawes talks with Morris about how hisn poetry is decidedly less political than most of his contemporaries that work mainly in a postcolonial vein of discourse.

657.   _____. "Claire Harris." *Talk Yuh Talk: Interviews with Anglophone Caribbean Poets.* Charlottesville, VA: University of Virginia Press, 2001. 61-72.

Claire Harris was born in 1937 in Trinidad. Now based in Canada (Calgary, Alberta), she devotes a great deal of her writing to topics that impact women of all ethnic, cultural, and racial backgrounds. Dawes spends most of the interview discussing Harris's emphasis on form in her writing.

658.   _____. "Olive Senior." *Talk Yuh Talk: Interviews with Anglophone Caribbean Poets.* Charlottesville, VA: University of Virginia Press, 2001. 73-85.

Olive Senior was born in 1941 in rural Jamaica. Now writing from Toronto, Canada, Senior maintains a Caribbean sensibility in her writing – poetry and short stories. In the interview Dawes questions Senior about her growth as a poet from her first collection (*Talking of Trees*) to her second collection (*Gardening in the Tropics*).

659.   _____. "Cyril Dabydeen." *Talk Yuh Talk: Interviews with Anglophone Caribbean Poets.* Charlottesville, VA: University of Virginia Press, 2001. 86-98.

Dabydeen was born in 1945 in a rural environment in Guyana. Educated in Canada, he has published over a dozen books, including fiction and poetry. In this interview, Dawes questions Dabydeen about the poetic emphasis in all of his writing and the overall development of his form.

660.   _____. "Lorna Goodison." *Talk Yuh Talk: Interviews with Anglophone Caribbean Poets.* Charlottesville, VA: University of Virginia Press, 2001. 99-107.

Lorna Goodison was born in Jamaica in 1947. Currently living in the United States, she continues to write and teach at the University of Michigan, Ann Arbor. She discusses her development as a writer with emphasis on her views as a woman and the influences of music and Rastafarianism on her writing.

661.   _____. "Ramabai Espinet." *Talk Yuh Talk: Interviews with Anglophone Caribbean Poets.* Charlottesville, VA: University of Virginia Press, 2001. 108-123.

Ramabai Espinet was born in 1948 in Trinidad. Primarily a poet, her work explores the outsider position of (East) Indians in the Caribbean. In her interview with Dawes she discusses how this issue informs her writing.

662.   _____. "John Robert Lee." *Talk Yuh Talk: Interviews with Anglophone Caribbean Poets.* Charlottesville, VA: University of Virginia Press, 2001. 124-134.

Lee was born in St. Lucia in 1948 and currently resides there. In the early 1970s, he was involved in the Rastafarian movement and later embraced Christianity. Dawes talks with Lee about the dominance of Christianity as a theme in his recent work and his relationship with Derek Walcott.

663.   _____. "Grace Nichols." *Talk Yuh Talk: Interviews with Anglophone Caribbean Poets.* Charlottesville, VA: University of Virginia Press, 2001. 135-147.

Grace Nichols was born in 1950 in Guyana. She moved to the United Kingdom where she distinguished herself as one of Britain's most prolific women poets. Nichols discusses her beginnings as a writer and the evolution of her writing techniques in this interview with Dawes.

664.   _____. "Lillian Allen." *Talk Yuh Talk: Interviews with Anglophone Caribbean Poets.* Charlottesville, VA: University of Virginia Press, 2001. 148-160.

Lillian Allen was born in Spanish Town, Jamaica in 1951. Educated in the United States, she moved to Canada and became involved with the dub poetry mode. Dawes talks to Allen about her development as a writer and performer in this genre.

665.   _____. "Kendel Hippolyte." *Talk Yuh Talk: Interviews with Anglophone Caribbean Poets.* Charlottesville, VA: University of Virginia Press, 2001. 161-172.

Kendel Hippolyte was born in St. Lucia in 1952. Educated at the University of the West Indies in Jamaica, he began to write, publish, and perform his poetry at this time. Dawes talks with Hippolyte about his writing techniques, early influences, and publishing venues.

666.   _____. "Jane King." *Talk Yuh Talk: Interviews with Anglophone Caribbean Poets.* Charlottesville, VA: University of Virginia Press, 2001. 173-182.

Jane King was born in St. Lucia in 1952. She is one of the founding members of the Lighthouse Theater Company along with her husband, Kendel Hippolyte. Dawes talks with King about her strong emphasis on form in her poetry and the things that influence her choice of subject matter.

667.   _____. "Opal Palmer Adisa." *Talk Yuh Talk: Interviews with Anglophone Caribbean Poets.* Charlottesville, VA: University of Virginia Press, 2001. 183-195.

Opal Palmer Adisa was born and grew up in Jamaica. Educated in America, she has published short stories, poetry collections, and one novel. Dawes talks with Adisa about the centrality of home (Jamaica) in her poetry and her womanist sensibility.

668.   _____. "David Dabydeen." *Talk Yuh Talk: Interviews with Anglophone Caribbean Poets.* Charlottesville, VA: University of Virginia Press, 2001. 196-214.

David Dabydeen was born in 1955 and grew up in the rural and urban areas of Guyana. He currently heads the Caribbean Studies Department at the University of Warwick. Dawes talks with Dabydeen about the emphasis on slavery and indenture in his writing in terms of understanding and writing about the present. Dabydeen also talks about the dualities in his work – writing about the heritages of the African and Indian past.

669.   _____. "Afua Cooper." *Talk Yuh Talk: Interviews with Anglophone Caribbean Poets.* Charlottesville, VA: University of Virginia Press, 2001. 215-225.

Afua Cooper was born in Jamaica in 1957. She later moved to Canada, studied history, and began to write. The interview begins with Dawes asking Cooper about the impact of the supernatural on her writing. She also talks about the 1970's as a period that shaped her life and writing due to the political, social, and economic turmoil of the period.

670.   _____. "Fred D'Aguiar." *Talk Yuh Talk: Interviews with Anglophone Caribbean Poets*. Charlottesville, VA: University of Virginia Press, 2001. 226-235.

Fred D'Aguiar was born in England to Guyanese parents and was sent to Guyana at an early age to be raised by his Grandmother. He returned to England at age thirteen and in 1985 he published his first collection of poetry. D'Aguiar talks with Dawes about the heavy British influences on his writing style. He also talks about the influences of certain Caribbean poets such as Derek Walcott, Wilson Harris (better known as a fiction writer), and Martin Carter.

671.   _____. *Talk Yuh Talk: Interviews with Anglophone Caribbean Poets*. Charlottesville, VA: University of Virginia Press, 2001.

Dawes' basic thesis for this collection of essays revolves around the balance of the influences on Caribbean writers of other Caribbean writers as well as the works of their colonial predecessors. This text is a collection of interviews with nineteen Caribbean poets.

672.   Hargus, Billy Bob. "Linton Kwesi Johnson." Interview. 1997. 16 May 2001 *http://www.furious.com/perfect/lkj.html*.

This is an interview with the poet Linton Kwesi Johnson – well-known for his pioneering style in dub poetry. Johnson talks about his early life in Jamaica, his move to England, global racism, poetry in Jamaica, and his development as a writer and performer.

673.   Hirsch, Edward. "The Art of Poetry (1986)." *Critical Perspectives on Derek Walcott*. Ed. Robert D. Hamner. Washington, D.C.: Three Continents Press, 1993. 65-83.

This interview was conducted over a three-day period on Walcott's home island of St. Lucia. His early life, influences, and work to the [then] present are discussed at length.

674.   Milne, Anthony. "Derek Walcott (1982)." *Critical Perspectives on Derek Walcott*. Ed. Robert D. Hamner. Washington, D.C.: Three Continents Press, 1993. 58-64.

This interview was conducted in Trinidad (1982) when Walcott was in the country to give a reading at the Royal Victoria Institute and to meet with members of the Trinidad Theatre Workshop. He discusses his work in America and the Caribbean and comments on the work of other Caribbean writers.

675.   Morris, Mervyn. "Mikey Smith, Dub Poet: Interviewed by Mervyn Morris." *Jamaica Journal* 18.2 (May-July 1985): 38-45.

This interview with Mikey Smith was conducted two years before he was stoned to death. Smith discusses his dub poetry/writing technique, performance versus the printed work, and his feelings about Rastafarianism.

676.   Munro, Ian H. and Reinhard W. Sander, eds. *Kas-Kas: Interviews with Three Caribbean Writers in Texas – George Lamming, C. L. R. James, Wilson Harris.* Austin, TX: African and Afro-American Research Institute, University of Texas, 1972.

These interviews with Lamming, James, and Harris were conducted over a two-year period when they conducted lectures and classes at the University of Texas at Austin. The interviews with Lamming and James are a combination of recorded material from class lectures, answers to student questions and meetings with editors Ian Munro and Reinhard Sander. The interview with Harris was gathered from a series of recorded meetings with the editors.

677.   Reid, Monty. "Choosing Control: An Interview with Claire Harris." *Waves: Fine Canadian Writing* 13.1 (1984): 37-41.

This interview was conducted early in Claire Harris's career as a poet. Harris comments on her approach to writing and overall philosophy.

678.   Rowell, Charles. "An Interview with Olive Senior." *Callaloo: An Afro-American and African Journal of Arts and Letters* 11.3 (1988): 480-490.

This interview was orchestrated through the mail during the period of March through May of 1988. Senior discusses a number of issues with Rowell – the motivating factors that made her write, her poetry and short stories, and the literary scene in Jamaica.

679.   Sanders, Leslie and Arun Mukherjee. "A Sense of Responsibility: An Interview with Claire Harris." *West Coast Line* 22.1 (1997): 26-37.

Harris discusses her writing from the standpoint of responsibility –
personal, cultural, and social. She reveals a great deal about her
development as a writer since the late 1970s through the early 1980s.

680.   Sinnewe, Dirk. "Derek Walcott Interviewed By Dirk Sinnewe." *The
Journal of Commonwealth Literature* 34.2 (1999): 1-7.

Walcott discusses why he writes in English rather than French Creole. He
also talks with Sinnewe about the overall state of Caribbean Literature. He
talks briefly about some of his plays.

681.   Williams, Emily Allen. "An Interview with Claire Harris." *Wasafiri* 32
(Autumn 2000): 41-44.

This interview with Harris took place at her home in Calgary. Harris'
discussion with Williams is chronological – from childhood through her
education up to her development as a writer. Harris speaks candidly about
the challenges of writing as a woman and a black person in Canada.

VII. Recorded Works (Audio and Audio-Visual)

682. Allen, Lillian. *Conditions Critical*. Toronto, Ontario: Verse to Vinyl Records, 1987.

Sound cassette.

683. _____. *De Dub Poets*. Curfew, 1985.

Sound cassette.

684. _____. *Let the Heart See*. 1987.

Sound cassette.

685. _____. *Nothing But A Hero*. Redwood, 1992.

Sound cassette.

686. _____. *Revolutionary Tea Party*. 1986.

Album.

687. _____. *(We Shall Take Our) Freedom & Dance*. Verse to Vinyl Records, 1989.

Album.

688.   Bennett, Louise. *Children's Jamaican Songs and Games*. Washington, DC: Smithsonian Folkways, 1992.

Sound cassette.

689.   _____. *Jamaica Labrish*. Sydney: ABC Radio, 1993.

Sound cassette.

690.   _____. *Miss Lou! Yes M'Dear*. Kingston, Jamaica: Sonic Sounds, 1982.

Compact disc.

691.   Berry, James and Alistair Bamford. *Benjamin Zephaniah, E.A. Markham, Amyrl Johnson, and David Dabydeen*. London: British Library National Sound Archive for Bluefoot Cassettes, 1989.

Sound cassette.

692.   Bovell, Dennis. *Dub Master*. JMA, 1995.

Compact disc.

693.   Brand, Dionne and Ginny Stikeman, prods. *Sisters in the Struggle*. Montreal, Canada: National Film Board, 1991.

Film reel/16 mm.

694.   Brathwaite, Edward Kamau. *Atumpan Sound Recording*. Washington, D.C.: Watershed Intermedia, 1989.

Sound cassette.

695.   Brathwaite, Kamau and Georgette M. Dorn. *Barbadian Poet Edward Kamau Brathwaite Reads From His Poetry and is Interviewed By Georgette M. Dorn*. Washington, DC: Library of Congress/Archive of Hispanic Literature on Tape, 1982.

Sound tape reel.

696.   Brathwaite, Kamau and Susan Stramberg. *Brathwaite*. Washington, DC: National Public Radio, 1988.

Sound cassette.

697.   Brathwaite, Kamau. *Edward Kamau Brathwaite Reading His Poems.*
        Washington, DC: Library of Congress/Archive of Recorded Poetry and
        Literature, 1982.

        Sound recording.

698.   Breeze, Jean "Binta". *Riding on de Riddym: Selected Spoken Works.* 57
        Productions, 1997.

        Sound cassette.

699.   _____. *Tracks* (with Dennis Bovell Dub Band). Shanachie, 1990.

        Compact disc.

700.   Bruner, Charlotte, et. al. *Anglophone and Francophone: Talks with and
        About Third World Writers.* Ames, Iowa: WOI Radio, 1979.

        Six sound cassettes.

701.   Chalkdust. *Drums of the Millenium.* 2000.

        Compact disc.

702.   _____. *Vintage Chalkdust.* 2001.

        Compact disc.

703.   Cudjoe, Selwyn. *Caribbean Women Writers: The First International Con-
        ference.* Banyan for Calaloux Publications, 1994.

        Videocassette of conference proceedings.

704.   Dabydeen, David, et. al. *Caribbean Poetry: The Literary and Oral Tradi-
        tions.* Northbrook, IL: Roland Films in Art, 1990.

        Videocassette of readings by Caribbean and West Indian poets.

705.   *The Dual Muse: Symposium on November 8-9, 1997, Washington Uni-
        versity/Steinberg Gallery/International Writers Center.* Saint Louis: Wash-
        ington University School of Art, 1997.

        Four videocassettes of conference proceedings; includes reading by
        Derek Walcott.

706.   Figueroa, John, ed. *Poets of the West Indies Reading Their Own Works.*
        New York: Caedmon, 1971.

        Sound cassette.

707.   Hall, Tony, Christopher Laird, and Bruce Paddington, prod. and dir.
        Independent Voices. Banyan Studios and UNESCO. Banyan: Crossbreed
        Productions, 1991.

        Videocassette of Caribbean writers.

708.   Johnson, Linton Kwesi. *Bass Culture.* Mango, 1980.

        Sound disc, 33 1/3 rpm.

709.   _____. *The Best of Linton Kwesi Johnson.* Epic, 1980.

        Sound cassette.

710.   _____. *Dread Beat An' Blood.* Frontline, 1977.

        Sound cassette.

711.   _____. *Dub Poetry.* Mango, 1985.

        Sound cassette.

712.   _____. *Forces of Victory.* Mango, 1979.

        Sound disc, 33 1/3 rpm.

713.   _____. *In Concert with the Dub Band (Live).* Shanachie, 1985.

        Sound cassette.

714.   _____. *In Dub, Vol. 2.* LKJ, 1994.

        Compact disc.

715.   _____. *Independent Intavenshan: The Island Anthology.* Island, 1998.

        Two compact discs.

716. _____. Linton Kwesi Johnson. Mango, 1985.

Compact disc.

717. _____. *LKJ Acappella Live*. LKJ Records, 1997.

Compact disc.

718. _____. *Making History*. Mango, 1984.

Compact disc.

719. _____. *More Time*. LKJ, 1999.

Compact disc.

720. _____. *Tings An' Times*. Shanachie, 1991.

Compact disc.

721. Keens-Douglas, Paul. *More of Me*. Port of Spain, 1987.

Sound cassette.

722. _____. *Stress an' Strain*. Port of Spain, 1995.

Sound cassette.

723. Lord Kitchener. *Vol. 1/Klassic Kitchener*. 2000.

Compact disc.

724. _____. *Vol. 2/ Klassic Kitchener*. 2000.

Compact disc.

725. Mad Professor. *Afrocentric Dub: Black Liberation Dub, Chapter 5*. ARW, 1998.

Compact disc.

726. _____. *Dubtronic*. ARW, 1998.

Compact disc.

727.   _____. *Fire in Dub*. ARW, 1998.

Compact disc.

728.   _____. *Lost Scrolls of Moses*. ARW, 1993.

Compact disc.

729.   _____. *Ras Portraits*. Ras, 1997.

Compact disc.

730.   Mandiela, Ahdri Zhina. *Barefoot and Black*. n.d.

Sound cassette.

731.   _____. *First and Last*. n.d.

Sound cassette.

732.   _____. *Step/Into My Hat*. n.d.

Sound cassette.

733.   Mighty Sparrow. *Christmas Ballads*. 2000.

Compact disc.

734.   _____. *Cokie Eye Rooster.* 1999.

Compact disc.

735.   _____. *Don't Touch The*. 1999.

Compact disc.

736.   _____. *Explodes Into Calypso Time*. 1996.

Compact disc.

737.   _____. *Guidance*. 2000.

Compact disc.

738.   ____. *Supreme.* 1999.

Compact disc.

739.   ____. *Top Gun.* 2000.

Compact disc.

740.   ____. *Vol. 2/Mighty Sparrow.* 2000.

Compact disc.

741.   ____. *Zesty.* 2000.

Compact disc.

742.   Mohabeer, Michele, prod. *Coconut, Cane and Cutlass.* New York: Third Eye Productions, 1994.

Videocassette of Indo-Caribbean women's lives and labor.

743.   Mutabaruka, Breeze, & Others. *Word Soun' 'Ave Power: Dub Poets and Dub.* Heartbeat Records, 1994.

Compact disc.

744.   Mutabaruka, Scientist & Others. *Dub Poets Dub.* Heartbeat Records, 1984.

Sound cassette.

745.   Nichols, Grace. *I is a Long Memoried Woman.* Produced by Ingrid Lewis. Directed by Frances Anne Soloman. New York: Women Make Movies, 1990.

Videocassette of lives of women from and in the Third World.

746.   Oku Onuora. *Dubbin' Away.* Roir, 1999.

Compact disc.

747.   ____. *I A Tell: Dubwize & Otherwise.* Roir, 1990.

Compact disc.

748.   _____. *New Jerusalem Dub*. Roir, 1990.

Sound cassette.

749.   _____. *Overdub: Tribute to King Tubby*. Ion, 2000.

Compact disc.

750.   Oku & AK7. *Pressure Drop*. Heartbeat, 1990.

Compact disc.

751.   Queen Majeeda. *Conscious*. Heartbeat Records, 1993.

Compact disc.

752.   Walcott, Derek. *Derek Walcott Reads*. New York: Cademon, 1994.

Sound cassette.

753.   _____. *Derek Walcott Reading His Poems*. Washington, DC: Library of Congress /Archive of Recorded Poetry and Literature, 1986.

Sound tape reel.

754.   _____. *Omeros*. Compass Films, 1990.

Videocassette.

755.   Walcott, Derek and Bill Moyers. *Derek Walcott*. Princeton, NJ: Films for the Humanities and Sciences, 1994.

Videocassette of interview done by Moyers.

756.   Walcott, Derek, Wayne Johnston Pond, and Tim McLaurin. *Walcott on Poetry*. Research Triangle Park, NC: National Humanities Center, 1995.

Compact disc.

757.   Walcott, Derek and Rebekah Presson. *Derek Walcott*. Kansas City, MO: University of Missouri, 1990.

Sound cassette of interview done by Presson.

758.   Walcott, Derek and Victor Questel. *Interview with Derek Walcott.* Port of
         Spain, Trinidad and Tobago: 1980.

         Two videocassettes.

759.   Walcott, Derek and Kenneth Ramchand. *Interview with Derek Walcott.*
         Port of Spain, Trinidad and Tobago, 1981.

         Two videocassettes.

760.   *West Indian Poetry.* San Fernando, Trinidad and Tobago, 1990.

         Sound cassette of readings by Martin Carter, Edward Brathwaite, Dennis
         Scott, and Ian McDonald.

761.   *Woman Talk: Caribbean Dub Poetry.* Heartbeat Records, 1986.

         Sound cassette of readings by female dub poets Afua Cooper, Anita
         Stewart, Louise Bennett, Cheryl Byron, and others.

762.   *Word Up.* Ontario: Virgin/EMI Music Canada, 1995.

         Compact disc of Canadian poets; features Lillian Allen.

763.   Zephaniah, Benjamin. *Back to Roots.* Acid Jazz, 1995.

         Compact disc.

764.   _____. *Belly of De Beast.* Ariwa, 1996.

         Compact disc.

765.   _____. *Big Boys Don't Make Girls Cry.* Upright, 1984.

         Sound cassette.

766.   _____. *Crisis.* Workers Playtime, 1992.

         Compact disc.

767.   _____. *Dub Ranting.* Radical Wallpaper, 1982.

         Sound cassette.

768.   _____. *Free South Africa.* Upright, 1986.

Sound cassette.

769.   _____. *Rasta LP.* Upright, 1983.

Sound cassette.

770.   _____. *US AN DEM.* Mango, 1990.

Sound recording/LP.

771.   _____. *Wicked World.* London: Penguin, 2000.

Sound cassette/Puffin audio-book series.

VIII. *Guide to Further Reading*

772.   Allen, Ray and Lois Wilcken. *Island Sounds in the Global City: Caribbean Popular Music and Identity in New York.* Urbana: University of Illinois Press, 2001.

773.   Alleyne, Mervyn. *Africa: Roots of Jamaican Culture.* Chicago, IL: Research Associates/School Times Publication, 1996.

774.   Anderson, Benedict. *Imagined Communities: Reflections on the Origin and Spread of Nationalism.* London; New York: Verso, 1991.

775.   Anozie, Sunday O. *Structural Models and African Poetics: Towards A Pragmatic View of Literature.* London: Routledge & Kegan Paul, 1981.

776.   Bailyn, Bernard. *The Peopling of British North America: An Introduction.* New York: Vintage Books, 1988.

777.   Barrett, L. *The Rastafarians: Sounds of Cultural Dissonance.* MA: Beacon Press, 1988.

778.   Barry, Chevannes. *Learning to Be A Man: Culture, Socialization and Gender Identity in Five Caribbean Communities.* Barbados: University of the West Indies Press, 2001.

779.   Beckles, Hillary. *Black Rebellion in Barbados: The Struggle Against Slavery, 1627-1838.* Bridgetown, Barbados: Antilles Publications, 1984.

780.   Bell, Roseann P., Bettye J, Parker, and Beverly Guy-Sheftall, eds. *Sturdy Black Bridges: Visions of Black Women in Literature.* New York: Anchor Press/Doubleday, 1979.

781.   Bickerton, Derek. *Dynamics of a Creole System*. New York: Cambridge University Press, 1975.

782.   Birbalsingh, Frank, ed. *Indenture and Exile: The Indo-Caribbean Experience*. Toronto: TSAR, 1989.

783.   Blackburn, Robin. *The Overthrow of Colonial Slavery, 1776-1848*. London; New York: Verso, 1988.

784.   Blackman, Margot. *Bajan Proverbs*. Montreal, 1982.

785.   Boon, James A. *Other Tribes, Other Scribes*. Cambridge; New York: Cambridge University Press, 1982.

786.   Brathwaite, Edward Kamau. *The Development of Creole Society in Jamaica, 1770-1820*. Oxford; New York: Oxford University Press, 1971.

787.   _____. *The Folk Culture of the Slaves in Jamaica*. London: New Beacon Books, 1981.

788.   _____. *Wars of Respect: Nanny and Sam Sharpe*. Kingston, Jamaica: API, 1977.

789.   Breitinger, Eckard and Reinhard Sander, eds. *Studies in Commonwealth Literature*. Tubingen: G. Narr Verlag, 1985.

790.   Brereton, Bridget. *Colonial Trinidad, 1870-1900*. Cambridge: Cambridge University Press, 1980.

791.   Bush, Barbara. *Slave Women in Caribbean Society, 1650-1838*. London: Heinemann Publishers, 1990.

792.   Campbell, Horace. *Rasta and Resistance: From Marcus Garvey to Walter Rodney*. Trenton, NJ: Africa World Press, 1987.

793.   Campbell, Mavis C. *The Maroons of Jamaica, 1655-1796*. Trenton, NJ: Africa World Press, 1990.

794.   Carnegie, Charles V. *Afro-Caribbean Villages in Historical Perspective*. Kingston: African-Caribbean Institute of Jamaica, 1987.

795.   Cassidy, Frederic. *Jamaica Talk: Three Hundred Years of the English Language in Jamaica.* London: Macmillan Education, 1982.

796.   Christian, Barbara. *Black Feminist Criticism: Perspectives on Black Women Writers.* New York: Pergamon Press, 1985.

797.   Clarke, Peter Bernard. *Black Paradise: The Rastafarian Movement.* CA: Borgo Press, 1988.

798.   Clifford, James. *The Predicament of Culture: Twentieth Century Ethnography, Literature, and Art.* Cambridge, MA: Harvard University Press, 1988.

799.   Collymore, Frank. *Barbadian Dialect.* Bridgetown, Barbados: Barbados National Trust, 1970.

800.   Coombs, Orde, ed. *Is Massa Day Dead?* New York: Anchor Books, 1974.

801.   Corsbie, Ken. *Theatre in the Caribbean.* London: Hodder & Stoughton, 1984.

802.   Crahan, Margaret E. and Franklin W. Knight, eds. *Africa and the Caribbean: The Legacies of A Link.* Baltimore: Johns Hopkins University Press, 1979.

803.   Craig, Susan, ed. *Contemporary Caribbean: A Sociological Reader.* 2 vols. Port of Spain, Trinidad: College Press, 1981-1982.

804.   Craton, Michael. *Testing the Chains: Resistance to Slavery in the British West Indies.* Ithaca: Cornell University Press, 1982.

805.   Crowley, Tony. *The Politics of Discourse: The Standard Language Question in British Cultural Debates.* London: Macmillan Education, 1989.

806.   Dalphinis, Morgan. *Caribbean and African Languages: Social History, Language, Literature, and Education.* London: Karia Press, 1985.

807.   Dawes, Neville. *Prolegomena to Caribbean Literature.* Kingston, Jamaica: Institute of Jamaica, 1977.

808.   D'Costa, Jean and Barbara Lalla, eds. *Voices in Exile: Jamaican Texts of the 18th and 19th Centuries.* Tuscaloosa, AL: University of Alabama Press, 1989.

809. _____, eds. *Language in Exile: Three Hundred Years of Jamaican Creole.* Tuscaloosa, AL: University of Alabama Press, 1990.

810. Devonish, Hubert. *Language and Liberation: Creole Language Politics in the Caribbean.* London: Karia Press, 1986.

811. Dobbin, Jay D. *The Jumbie Dance of Montserrat: A Study of Trance Ritual in the West Indies.* Ohio State University Press, 1986.

812. Elgersman, Maureen G. *Unyielding Spirits: Black Women and Slavery in Early Canada and Jamaica.* New York: Garland Publishing, 1999.

813. Gorlach, Manfred and John A. Holm, eds. *Focus on the Caribbean.* PA: J. Benjamins, 1986.

814. Goveia, Elsa V. *The West Indian Slave Laws of the Eighteenth Century.* London, 1970.

815. Griffiths, Gareth. *A Double Exile: African and West Indian Writing Between Two Cultures.* London: Boyars, 1978.

816. Harlow, Barbara. *Resistance Literature.* New York: Methuen, 1987.

817. Harris, Wilson. *History, Fable, and Myth in the Caribbean and Guianas.* Edgar Mittelholzer Memorial Lecture. Georgetown, Guyana: National History and Arts Council, 1970.

818. Havelock, Eric Alfred. *The Muse Learns to Write: Reflections on Orality and Literacy from Antiquity to the Present.* New Haven, CT: Yale University Press, 1986.

819. Holm, John. *Pidgins and Creoles: Theory and Structure.* Cambridge; New York: Cambridge University Press, 1988.

820. hooks, bell. *Feminist Theory From Margin to Center.* Boston, MA: South End Press, 1984.

821. Hulme, Peter. *Colonial Encounters: Europe and the Native Caribbean 1492-1797.* London: Routledge, 1986.

822. Hymes, D. L., ed. *Pidginization and Creolization of Languages.* Cambridge: Cambridge University Press, 1974.

823.   Inikori, J. E., ed. *Forced Exile: The Impact of the Forced Slave Trade on African Societies.* New York, 1982.

824.   Jonas, Joyce. *Anancy in the Great House: Ways of Reading West Indian Fiction.* New York: Greenwood Press, 1990.

825.   Kerns, Virginia. *Women and the Ancestors: Black Carib Kinship and Ritual.* IL: University of Illinois Press, 1989.

826.   Klein, Herbert S. *The Middle Passage: Comparative Studies of the Atlantic Slave Trade.* Princeton, NJ: Princeton University Press, 1978.

827.   Knight, Franklin W. *The Caribbean: The Genesis of a Fragmented Nationalism.* New York: Oxford University Press, 1990.

828.   Le Page, Robert Brock and Andree Tabouret-Keller. *Acts of Identity: Creole-Based Approaches to Language and Ethnicity.* New York: Cambridge University Press, 1985.

829.   Lewis, Gordon K. *The Growth of the Modern West Indies.* London, 1983.

830.   _____. *Mainstreams of Caribbean Thought.* Baltimore, 1985.

831.   Lowenthal, David and Lambros Comitas, eds. *Consequences of Class and Color: West Indian Perspectives.* New York: Anchor Books, 1973.

832.   Mair, Lucille Mathurin. *The Rebel Woman in the British West Indies During Slavery.* Kingston, Jamaica: Institute of Jamaica Publications Ltd., 1995.

833.   Marable, Manning. *African and Caribbean Politics: From Kwame Nkrumah to the Grenada Revolution.* London: Verso, 1987.

834.   McCartney, Timothy O. *Ten, Ten, the Bible Ten: Obeah in the Bahamas.* Nassau: Timpaul Publications, 1976.

835.   _____. *Women Field Workers in Jamaica During Slavery.* Kingston, Jamaica: University of the West Indies, 1987.

836.   Mintz, Sidney W., ed. *Slavery, Colonialism, and Racism.* New York: Norton, 1975.

837.   _____. *Sweetness and Power: The Place of Sugar in Modern History*. Harmondsworth, 1985.

838.   Mintz, Sidney W. and Sally Price, eds. *Caribbean Contours*. Baltimore, 1985.

839.   Mordecai, Martin and Pamela Mordecai. *Culture and Customs of Jamaica*. Westport, CT: Greenwood Press, 2001.

840.   Murrell, Nathaniel S. *Religion, Culture, and Tradition in the Caribbean*. Basingstoke: Macmillan, 2000.

841.   Nettleford, Rex. *Identity, Race, and Protest in Jamaica*.   New York: Morrow, 1972.

842.   _____. *Inward Stretch, Outward Reach: A Voice From the Caribbean*. New York: Caribbean Diaspora Press/Medgar Evers College, 1995.

843.   Ngugi wa Thiong'o. *Homecoming: Essays on African and Caribbean Literature, Culture, and Politics*. London: Heinemann, 1972.

844.   Nicholas, Tracy. *Rastafari: A Way of Life*. New York: Anchor Books, 1979.

845.   Osei, Gabriel Kingsley. *Caribbean Women: Their History and Habits*. London: African Publication Society, 1979.

846.   Ottley, Carlton Robert. *Creole Talk of Trinidad and Tobago*. 4th ed. Diego Martin, Trinidad/Tobago: Crusoe, 1981.

847.   Owens, J. *Dread: The Rastafarians of Jamaica*. Exeter, NH: Heinemann, 1982.

848.   Oxaal, Ivar. *Black Intellectuals and the Dilemmas of Race and Class in Trinidad*. MA: Schenkman, 1982.

849.   Parry, John, Philip Sherlock, and Anthony Maingot. *A Short History of the West Indies*. 4th ed. London: Macmillan Caribbean, 1987.

850.   Pereira, J.R., ed. *Caribbean Literature in Comparison*.   Kingston, Jamaica: Institute of Caribbean Studies, 1990.

851.   Petersen, Kirsten Holt and Anna Rutherford, eds. *A Double Colonization: Colonial and Post-Colonial Women's Writing.* Mundelstrup, Denmark: Dangaroo Press, 1986.

852.   Philip, M. Nourbese. *Frontiers and Writings in Racism and Culture.* Stratford, Ontario: Mercury Press, 1992.

853.   Poynting, Jeremy. *The Second Shipwreck: Indo-Caribbean Literature.* London: Hansib, 1988.

854.   Price, Richard, ed. *Maroon Societies: Rebel Slave Communities in the Americas.* Baltimore: Johns Hopkins University Press, 1987.

855.   Rickford, John R. *Dimensions of a Creole Continuum: History, Texts, and Linguistic Analysis of Guyanese Creole.* CA: Stanford University Press, 1987.

856.   _____. *A Festival of Guyanese Words.* 2nd ed. Georgetown: University of Guyana, 1978.

857.   Roberts, Peter A. *West Indians and Their Language.* Cambridge; New York: Cambridge University Press, 1988.

858.   Searle, Chris. *Words Unchained: Language and Revolution in Grenada.* NJ: Zed Books, 1984.

859.   Senior, Olive. *A-Z of Jamaican Heritage.* Kingston, Jamaica: Heinemann Educational Books, 1987.

860.   _____. *Working Miracles: Women's Lives in the English-Speaking Caribbean.* Bloomington, IN, 1991.

861.   Sherlock, Philip. *West Indian Nations: A New History.* New York: St. Martin's Press, 1973.

862.   Sherlock, Philip and Rex Nettleford. *The University of the West Indies: A Caribbean Response to the Challenge of Change.* London: Macmillan Caribbean, 1990.

863.   Simpson, George Eaton. *Religious Cults of the Caribbean: Trinidad, Jamaica, and Haiti.* Rio Piedras, P.R.: Institute of Puerto Rico, University of Puerto Rico, 1980.

864.   Smith, Barbara Fletchman. *Mental Slavery: Psychoanalytic Studies of Caribbean People.* London: Rebus Press, 2000.

865.   Smith, Rowland. *Postcolonializing the Commonwealth: Studies in Literature and Culture.* Waterloo, Ontario: Wilfrid Laurier University Press, 2000.

866.   Stone, Carl. *Class, State, and Democracy in Jamaica.* New York: Praeger, 1986.

867.   Tanna, Laura. *Jamaican Folk Tales and Oral Histories.* Miami, FL: DLT Associates, 2000.

868.   Taylor, Patrick. *Nation Dance: Religion, Identity, and Cultural Difference in the Caribbean.* Bloomington: Indiana University Press, 2001.

869.   Temko, Florence and Randall Gooch. *Traditional Crafts from the Caribbean.* Minneapolis: Lerner Publications Co., 2001.

870.   Todd, Loreto. *Pidgins and Creoles.* London: Routledge, 1990.

871.   Williams, Joseph John. *Psychic Phenomena of Jamaica.* Westport, CT: Greenwood Press, 1979.

872.   _____. *Voodoos and Obeahs: Phases of West Indian Witchcraft.* New York: AMS Press, 1970.

873.   Wilson, Samuel M., ed. *The Indigenous People of the Caribbean.* Gainesville: University Press of Florida, 1999.

874.   Wooding, Charles J. *Evolving Culture: A Cross-Cultural Study of Suriname, West Africa, and the Caribbean.* Washington, DC: University Press of America, 1981.

Author Index

The numbers in this index refer to entry numbers, not page numbers, in the bibliography.

Title Index

The numbers in this index refer to entry numbers, not page numbers, in the bibliography.

Subject Index

The numbers in this index refer to entry numbers, not page numbers, in the bibliography.

About the Author

EMILY ALLEN WILLIAMS is Assistant Professor of English at Morehouse College and has been a Lecturer at the University of the West Indies.